A Fresh Approach to
Teaching Punctuation

HELPING YOUNG WRITERS
USE CONVENTIONS WITH
PRECISION AND PURPOSE

BY JANET ANGELILLO
FOREWORD BY LUCY McCORMICK CALKINS

S C H O L A S T I C
PROFESSIONAL BOOKS

NEW YORK • TORONTO • LONDON • AUCKLAND • SYDNEY • MEXICO CITY
NEW DELHI • HONG KONG • BUENOS AIRES

To Isoke Titilayo Nia
who, more than anyone, taught me
about punctuation and about teaching

Cover and foreword photographs by Vicky Kasala
Cover design by Vito Zarkovic
Interior design by Holly Grundon
Interior photographs by James Levin

ISBN 0-439-22245-1
Copyright © 2002 by Janet Angelillo
All rights reserved.
Printed in the U.S.A.

1 2 3 4 5 6 7 8 9 10   40   09 08 07 06 05 04 03 02

Contents

Acknowledgments

I am deeply indebted to all my colleagues at the Columbia University Teachers College Reading and Writing Project. It is impossible to separate where their thinking ends and mine begins, nor does my work exist apart from their influence. It was one Thursday, as we sat together in the Project library writing about an orange peel on our table, and playing with commas and semi-colons to make our writing clearer, that this work began.

At the Project, special thanks go to Carl Anderson, whose few words bring insights every week; Laurie Pessah, who believes that what we all need is a good listening to; and Kathleen Tolan, whose tireless work influences all our thinking. I especially thank Isoke Titilayo Nia, who studied punctuation with me and who was the first to shape my ideas as we prepared together for a Calendar Day at the College. Many thanks to Gaby Layden, for her support and commiseration, and to Leah Mermelstein, who tried out this approach and told me it works! Thanks also to Katie Ray of Western Carolina University. Most of all, I thank Lucy McCormick Calkins; without her and the unique community she has created at the Project, this work and this book would not exist.

Many thanks to the teachers who allowed me into their classrooms to work with their students: Aliza Konig, Minette Junkins, Kim Ethun, and Rachel Bard from P.S. 165 in Manhattan; Rob Ross, Marilyn Lopez, and Grace Heske from P.S. 206 in Queens; Leslie Feldman, Marie Kupillas, Hope Beyer, and Karen Kessler from P.S. 21 in Queens; Lisa Duffy and Roseanna Vallario from P.S. 96 in the Bronx; Lisa Castle from Parkway School in Plainview; and the middle school teachers from Community School District 26 in Queens. I could not name all the dedicated, smart teachers and principals who graciously invited me in, but I thank each and every one.

Many thanks to my faithful and tireless editors at Scholastic: Kate Montgomery, who made many insightful suggestions, Wendy Murray, whose gentle prodding and wise reading kept me going, and Raymond Coutu, whose careful, precise editing helped me say what I meant to say. Thanks to Phoebe Cottingham, Carol Bogen, Liz Meller, Meredith Downey, Connie Baird, Margot Ward, and the members of the Wednesday group at Chappaqua Meeting. They held me up many times when I thought I might fall down.

Finally, thanks to Cheryl, Mark, and Alex, who always make me laugh, especially when I get too serious, and to Ruby, Java, Sammy, Figgy, Lulu, Annie, and Bailey for making me play every day. Mostly, thanks to Charles, who believes in me, and built me a room of my own.

Foreword

"I love the whole idea of a writing workshop," teachers tell me. "But, but, but…" Their voices trail off. Then, with a gulp of resolve, they press on. "What about the skills?"

How glad I am that Janet Angelillo has written a book that enables us to respond by saying, loud and clear, that we needn't choose between teaching craftsmanship and teaching skills. Although we who write about empowering young people to craft their work have said all along that punctuation matters, we haven't yet given teachers the tools they need to teach punctuation well. Instead, we've gone on to write books filled with ideas for teaching children to write with detail, to show not tell, to emulate authors. But with this book, Janet has bravely broken that pattern, showing that, yes indeed, teachers who embrace writing workshop care about teaching the semicolon, the comma, and all the complex little pieces that sometimes intimidate children and adults alike. She brings us strategies to invigorate our classrooms with the excitement of discovery and the sheer power of language.

Punctuation may appear to be a small detail compared to the weighty matters of structure, theme, organization, and craft. Paradoxically, though, this least-celebrated portion of the literacy curriculum is the key to complex sentence structure and complex thinking. Punctuation is what links ideas together, what writers use to enfold and, in turn, express layered thoughts with clarity and grace. Teachers who want to empower young people to craft memoirs, poems, and book reviews also need to empower them to use subordinate clauses, make parenthetical remarks, and connect sentences with commas and semicolons. Janet shows how we can use methods that have helped children write with voice and detail to provide a full set of written-language tools.

I couldn't have chosen a better person to write this book. Janet is, first of all, a leader in literacy education. She has been a middle-school English teacher, a first-grade teacher, a department chairperson...and everything in between. For the past six years, she's been a leader among the Teachers College Reading and Writing Project staff, helping schools across New York City and the nation develop rigorous reading and writing curricula. This work allows Janet to situate her focus on punctuation into the context in which it belongs. In her book, punctuation instruction is nestled alongside literature circles, writers' notebooks, big books, and conferring. The writing is clear and concise, a model for all that she would have us share with our students. It is informed by the research advanced by scholars such as Brian Cambourne and Mina Shaughnessy. Janet is at once practical and progressive. Her book is a simple, elegant guide to planning and conducting a yearlong study of punctuation, integrated into a workshop curriculum.

Janet has filled bookcases in her kitchen, dining room, bedroom, and attic. Her living room feels like the reading room in a library. She is always finding books, recommending books, falling in love with books. And now this richly literate teacher of reading and writing has written a book filled with astute, informed, heartfelt ideas for teaching young people to write with clarity, and to use turns of phrase to establish emphasis and add color, texture, and nuance to their writing. I love this book, its author, and the new and exciting ideas here for us to share.

Lucy McCormick Calkins

Professor of Curriculum and Teaching at
Teachers College, Columbia University

Author of *The Art of Teaching Writing* and
The Art of Teaching Reading

Introduction

The Theory Behind My Thinking

Once I heard a story about Oscar Wilde. It seems he went to a dinner party where someone asked him how he was. "I'm exhausted," Wilde supposedly replied. "I spent the entire morning putting a comma in and the afternoon taking it out."

Sometimes it seems that punctuation is just as tedious and exhausting for our students. But apart from its obvious humor, the Wilde anecdote shows something important: Careful use of punctuation is more than simply applying a series of memorized rules. Wilde—certainly an accomplished writer—struggled to get the right punctuation into his writing, not to obey rules, but to communicate meaning to his readers.

Punctuation is part of a repertoire of good writing skills. It is one of many tools writers use for communicating meaning, along with word choice, thoughtful organization, a gripping lead, a satisfying ending, tension for pulling the reader along, and a host of others (Calkins, 1994; Fletcher, 1993; Murray, 1998). Writers use punctuation to shape the way readers read their texts. The system of little symbols we know as punctuation is full of meaning, nuance, and intricacy. It helps writing make sense to readers; it allows us to control the pace and volume and rhythm of the words. Used wisely, it is an invaluable writing tool.

The premise of this book is that we can teach students to use punctuation effectively and, in the process, use it correctly. We can do this if we nudge children toward discovering what punctuation does for readers in their reading and writers in their writing.

In the reading and writing work in many American schools, teachers acknowledge that the making of meaning is what matters most. But the teaching practice in many classrooms often does not match what we know about how children learn best. In some ways, the theories of cognitive psychologists and educational researchers do not inform enough of what we do, particularly how we teach written language conventions. In these days of high-stakes testing and accountability, we must be sure that we are looking at more than what we teach. We must also look at how we teach it. We must teach so children retain what we've taught them. The question, of course, is how will we do this? How do we teach so all children will learn? One way is to set up classrooms that are based on careful assessment of what children know, that honor their needs, and that allow us to build on learning from there. This book examines some ways you might do that.

Cambourne
Establishing Conditions for Learning

When we think about teaching punctuation, it is helpful to place it in a context of what we know about good teaching in general. We can look at the research of noted Australian researcher Brian Cambourne (1998) and apply it to teaching punctuation.

Cambourne delineates conditions he believes must be present in order for children to learn. His theory has been widely studied and implemented in Australia,

Cambourne's General Principles

◆ **Immersion:** Students must have the opportunity to read many types of texts. These can include books and periodicals provided by the teacher or chosen by the students, as well as environmental print around the room. Students must be thoroughly immersed in the type of text they are going to write.

◆ **Demonstration:** The teacher demonstrates to students, by using artifacts or actions, how reading and writing are done. He or she discusses print conventions with the students and provides opportunities for them to use print and see it being used. When the teacher thinks out loud, it helps students make meaning from the demonstration.

◆ **Expectations:** The teacher communicates positive expectations for success, implicitly and explicitly. He or she expects all students to succeed, and achieving that success is not negotiable.

◆ **Responsibility:** The teacher permits students to decide what they write, and when and how it will be written. By allowing students to make decisions about which piece of the language puzzle they tackle, the teacher helps them become independent learners.

◆ **Approximation:** Students approximate, or attempt to copy, the adult model. Errors are expected and are, in fact, important for growth. Learners make and test hypotheses, which may prove incorrect.

◆ **Practice:** The teacher provides opportunities to engage in reading or writing, giving students ample practice in developing skills. There is a block of time for reading and writing every day.

◆ **Engagement:** Students engage with print and with the teacher's demonstrations. They need to feel capable of doing what is taught, and confident that mistakes will be accepted without ridicule. This point is at the core of the learning process, because no learning will occur unless the learner is engaged.

◆ **Response:** Students and teacher exchange thoughts and feelings during whole-class instruction and individual conferences. These exchanges must be relevant, honest, non-punitive, and readily applied, with no strings attached.

and has influenced many of the ideas in this book. Eight conditions are at the core of his thinking:

- Immersion
- Demonstration
- Expectations
- Responsibility
- Approximation
- Practice
- Engagement
- Response

Although Cambourne's work is based on his research in preschool and the primary grades, the conditions he believes must be present for learning apply at every level. In fact, I keep them at the heart of my teaching in middle school. The emphasis is on the process of learning more than on the product of the learning. This is not to say that the product is not important—children must be able to produce writing that others can read. But teaching them how to learn is extremely important. In order to teach effectively, we must consider how to create Cambourne's conditions in our classrooms and how to teach punctuation in accordance with them. Classrooms must be founded on trust, routine, and ritual in order to establish comfortable places for learning (Peterson, 1992). We must create classrooms where children feel safe to explore and practice, and where there is latitude for making errors as they strive to improve in any skill, including the effective and correct use of punctuation.

Shaughnessy and Weaver

Looking at Errors and Stages of Learning

Mina P. Shaughnessy (1977) tells us in her book *Errors and Expectations* that errors say a great deal about the ways a student is gesturing toward new learning. Whenever we attempt to broaden our knowledge, we make errors in our early attempts. Therefore, a child attempting to write complex sentences can be expected to make more mistakes than if he or she stayed in the comfortable domain of writing simple sentences.

These errors should be regarded as evidence of growth, regardless of what the student is learning. So why do we accept errors on the road toward growth in, say, music, but are less likely to in writing? We would never dream of telling the budding violinist that he can't move up to a Mozart sonata because he'll make mistakes learning it, but we cringe when children make "mistakes" while writing. Shaughnessy's work helps us learn to look carefully at children's work, studying it to uncover information about their thinking processes. What may appear to be an error is often a milestone on the way toward a new skill or evidence of lack of experience—experience that we, as teachers, can provide young writers.

Constance Weaver, who studied teaching grammar in context (1990), agrees that errors reveal much about what children are learning. She recommends shifting from a behaviorist view of learning, which focuses on errors as mistakes, to a constructivist view, which sees errors as opportunities for learning. Weaver's work parallels Cambourne's because of its emphasis on practice, demonstration, and engagement.

Teachers who take a constructivist view focus on offering support as children try to make meaning from written symbols. The freedom they allow for mistakes in grammar and punctuation is similar to the freedom they allow when children are learning oral language. A small child's mistakes with oral language are not ridiculed, but are, rather, an accepted part of continued efforts to figure out the puzzle of oral language. We expect all children will eventually speak clearly and correctly. We must expect that they will read, write, spell, and punctuate clearly and correctly also, all in due time and under the proper conditions.

Graves and Calkins

Creating a Context for Constructing Knowledge

Researcher Donald Graves has greatly influenced the way we teach writing. Graves advocates having a writing workshop in which children are engaged in writing on self-generated topics, and where the teacher offers strategies for getting ideas, drafting, revising, and editing. In a workshop setting, children conduct inquiries into topics such as the punctuation inquiries I suggest in this book. While the teacher is very much at the helm, carefully assessing and coaching, the students themselves take responsibility for their learning.

Lucy Calkins (1997) teaches us that helping children to manage their own learning is a life lesson as well as a school lesson. When we help children become independent learners, it yields results for the rest of their lives. Calkins has spent many years studying reading and writing. Again and again, she has seen that interaction with authentic texts, as well as regular, systematic practice in reading and writing, are critical to helping children improve (Calkins, 2001). Children must be engaged. If they care about their work, they will have a purpose for using the strategies we teach them. And regular time for reading and writing every day is essential for student growth (Calkins, 1994).

When it comes to writing, Calkins feels that students must first learn to write "unselfconsciously." She says, "What matters . . . is that children get a feel for linking sentences and embedding phrases, for using symbols to encode the sounds of their voices. The use of the English language is a skill to be developed, not content to be taught, and it is best learned through active and purposeful experience with it." (Calkins, 1994).

Learning happens best when teachers create the conditions for children to construct their own knowledge. Under those circumstances, children do not depend on adults to disseminate information to them; with an adult's coaching, they can learn to figure things out for themselves. In this book, you will see some ways children can inquire deeply about punctuation and, in the process, come to own their learning.

Rosenblatt

Transacting With Readers

L ouise Rosenblatt (1978) wrote that all reading is a transaction between the text and the reader. The reader makes sense of the text based on past experience, present interests, or preoccupations. Language is social, individual, and certainly transactional; reading is an exemplification of the transactional nature of all human activity. Rosenblatt says:

"The speaker, it is often pointed out, offers many nonverbal cues to the listener, for example, through emphasis, pitch, inflection, rhythm, and, if face-to-face, facial expression and gesture. The writer thus must seek verbal substitutes for these. Hence the reader . . . finds it necessary to construct the speaker, the author—the voice, the tone, the rhythms and inflections, the persona—*as part of what he decodes from the text.* The relation with the author in actuality becomes a transaction between the reader and the author's text." (p. 20, italics added by author.)

When we teach students to use punctuation, we teach them a way to transact with their readers, a way to use dots and symbols to translate their voices to the page. Writing is no longer flat and dull. Students come to understand the code that will shape their internal voices as they orchestrate the reading of their writing.

Punctuation cannot save poor writing. But it will bring luster and personality, as well as clarity, to good writing. It is a powerful tool in the writer's hand and the reader's eye. We owe it to students to show them how powerful it is.

CHAPTER 1

Planning for a Year of Punctuation Work

*I*t's a glorious late October morning, and I'm climbing the stairs to Lisa Duffy's third-grade classroom on the fourth floor of an early twentieth-century school in New York City. On my way, I pass hallways filled with the sounds of children. I see pumpkin projects hanging from bulletin boards. I pass open classroom doors and see students inside, busy at tables and on rugs, writing and reading from books, charts, and stick-on notes, working with each other.

In my work as a literacy staff developer for the Teachers College Reading and Writing Project, I see scenes like these scores of times each week, scenes of teachers leading their students into the immense satisfaction of literate lives. I think about the reading and writing classrooms my colleagues and I are working hard to establish, and I think about the excitement and expectation students and teachers share when reading and writing change the way they live together in classrooms.

But when Lisa greets me at the classroom door, I'm reminded that this journey has its challenges as well as its rewards. She has a student's notebook open in her hand and a look of frustration on her face.

"It's unbelievable," she says, pointing to the child's work. "This is one of my best students. But look at this writing—no punctuation!"

I take a quick look at the child's notebook. Sure enough, there is a capital letter at the beginning of the first word on each page and a period after the last word on each page. Nothing else. No commas, no question marks, no quotation marks. Just a sea of words strung together for the reader to decipher.

Lisa leads me to a stack of notebooks on the round table near her classroom library. "I'm reading these while the kids are at math lab. I'm trying to assess their work and decide where to go next. Look, in one book after another it's the same thing: little or no punctuation. And I know they learned it before, because I taught it to them."

Lisa shakes her head and sighs. She has "looped" with her class, meaning she's followed them from second to third grade. So she knows what they learned last year. She knows she taught them periods and capitals and commas. But like so many other teachers, she is baffled by the way her teaching often doesn't "stick." She is baffled by the way her students, who know the routines and expectations of reading and writing workshop, do not use written language conventions in their writing. And she is worried because she knows that, without punctuation, their writing will never be precise and powerful.

"I really would like to study this," she says. "I want to figure out how to teach it so they will learn it and use it."

I smile and nod. Lisa has hit upon one thing that plagues many of us teachers: We teach something to our students, but they don't learn it. They don't hold on to it and make it part of their reading or writing lives. How can we get our teaching to last, we wonder? How can we teach children that what they learn in school fits into the important puzzle of their lives? And, specifically, how can we teach children to write to the best of their capabilities, using everything we have taught them about qualities of good writing, including accurate use of

Spotlight on Research

Recall Cambourne's eight conditions for learning described on page 9. The most important one, in my opinion, is engagement. If children are not engaged with the work, they will not learn it. It must matter to them.

written language conventions, in a consistent and purposeful way? Could it be that we have been going about teaching conventions in a way that is inconsistent with our other beliefs about teaching?

I think about the teaching of punctuation in the context of many classrooms. What happens, it seems, is that, while teachers are working hard to make children aware of the importance of using written language conventions, those conventions are often taught in the same ways educators have taught them for years. As a result, children are not becoming wise, or even proficient, at using conventions to help them express in writing their thoughts and ideas.

I turn from the notebooks to Lisa. "I agree with you. Whatever we are doing isn't working. I know that we learned punctuation when we went to school, but, somehow, many of the ways that worked for us don't work anymore."

Some General Beliefs About Thinking and Learning

I have strong beliefs about how children learn best. In reading and writing classrooms, students are co-learners with their teachers. Working together, they create communities where all students' learning is valued, and where the thinking behind an answer or product is as important as the result itself. They must work without anxiety, and feel free to make mistakes as they master something new. I also believe that children learn best when they:

◆ are active participants in inquiry

◆ study quality literature they grow to know well

◆ observe what experienced writers do

◆ have many opportunities to experiment with and apply their learning

"Let's think about this honestly," Lisa answers. "We know those ways worked for us, because we became teachers. After all, we like this stuff! But we'll never know how many people didn't get it, classmates of ours who still don't know when to use commas. I don't think we can assume that the old ways—the worksheets, drills, exercises from books—worked that well."

"You have a point," I reply. "In fact, as a learner, I don't think memorizing rules helped me internalize punctuation at all. But, as a writer, I think about how punctuation shapes the meaning of what I write and helps me clarify what I want to say."

"Maybe that's it!" Lisa says. "We have to teach children that writers have reasons for using punctuation. They must understand the thinking behind the rules."

"Yes," I answer. "The rules made little sense to me until I had something I wanted to say that I wanted others to read and understand. The difference was having intentions as a writer."

So Lisa and I agree that the teaching of written language conventions must be embedded in the children's intentions as writers, in their care about their writing and their audience, and in their desire to have readers read their writing in a certain way.

Lisa and I agree that using conventions must be a primary act of composition. That is, writers use punctuation to shape meaning as they write, and we need to find ways to help children think about doing their writing with the punctuation in it. We spend the next half-hour thinking and planning together and begin to think about some bottom-line expectations we should have for our instruction in order for punctuation to "count."

Thinking About New Ways to Teach Punctuation

After my conversation with Lisa, I begin to think constantly about punctuation—in every school I visit, including those in the suburbs and in other urban areas. I think about it as I sit with my colleagues at the Teachers

College Reading and Writing Project, especially with Isoke Nia who is a constant help to me. I think about it as I read professional books, especially those like *Wondrous Words* by Katie Wood Ray, that help me look at punctuation in a new way.

I see similar problems in so many classrooms that I realize it isn't just Lisa's problem. There is something awry in the way we are teaching conventions. In spite of the endless drills, ubiquitous editing sheets, peer editors, and room charts, student accuracy remains poor. Again and again, teachers are reluctant to display student writing because the lack or misuse of punctuation is embarrassing. They fear administrators and parents will mistakenly conclude that the lack of punctuation accuracy means teachers do not teach or value it. Yet these teachers care deeply about writing and about their students. They care deeply about examining their own practice and finding ways to give children tools to help them express themselves better. It seems counterproductive to worry about why the "old ways" do not seem to be effective. What matters is finding new and more effective ways to reach children, rather than grousing about the "good old days" when students supposedly learned punctuation easily.

TEACHING WITHIN THE WORKSHOP PHILOSOPHY

In the classrooms I visit, teachers follow a workshop philosophy (Atwell, 2000; Calkins, 1994). This includes having authentic purposes for writing and time to write in school. Writing grows from the children's ideas and life experiences. Students keep these ideas in notebooks as a basis for developing and exploring their ideas, much the way a scientist might grow a theory from field notes. They write drafts, revise using deliberate strategies, and publish regularly and often. Children write every day. They know writing is important—so important that it is at the center of their learning. In the reading workshop, students are reading authentic literature every day under the teacher's guidance. Reading and writing workshops provide the foundation for the kinds of active engagement and creative thinking we want children to develop.

The structure of the workshop is straightforward:

Mini-Lesson

Every day the class gathers together for a five- to ten-minute mini-lesson that is clear, precise, and often rehearsed. The mini-lesson is usually part of a related string of mini-lessons that, in turn, is part of a larger unit of study (Ray, 2001). A short lesson is effective because it can be tailored to specific class needs and doesn't take up much precious work time. The lesson topic arises from expectations for working up to a set of standards from the teacher's knowledge bank, and from daily assessment of student work.

Work Time and Conferences

After the mini-lesson, students go off to read or write for an extended time. It is extremely effective to teach something clearly and then immediately ask children to use it. While students are working, the teacher confers with students individually or in small groups as needed (Anderson, 2000). Careful notes of these conferences are kept to inform teaching and build curriculum. Students are held accountable for what they are taught in conferences, and teachers use these notes to plan powerful, specific, direct teaching.

Class Share

At the end of the work time, the class comes together again to share. It is not a time for the boldest students to showcase their work, but, rather, a time for the class to think further about its writing or prepare for writing to be done at home or

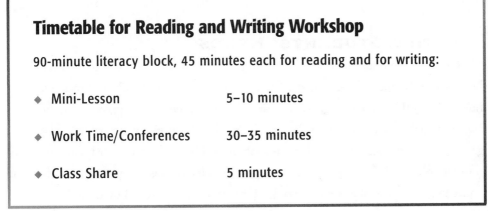

Timetable for Reading and Writing Workshop

90-minute literacy block, 45 minutes each for reading and for writing:

◆ Mini-Lesson	5–10 minutes
◆ Work Time/Conferences	30–35 minutes
◆ Class Share	5 minutes

the next day. It is teaching time. I might ask someone to share what I taught him or her in a conference. Or I might ask a child to share any new thinking he or she has done, or the use of an effective revision strategy. Class share is a time for pushing learning further, a time for giving writers something new to think about.

Laying the Foundation for a Punctuation Study

*I*t is often said that the best way to learn something is to teach it. Focusing my teaching on punctuation forced me to refresh my own knowledge. Armed with dusted-off copies of favorite books (see references), as well as new discoveries, I embarked on this journey of rethinking my teaching of conventions by reviewing the "old rules" I know so well. What I learned surprised me. The journey was anything but conventional, and the teachers who agreed to go along with me were committed to finding answers to our question. They included Marilyn Lopez and Rob Ross, who teach fourth and fifth grades respectively in Queens; Aliza Konig, who teaches third grade in Manhattan; and, of course, Lisa Duffy, in the Bronx. These teachers are all dedicated to their students and to the art of teaching. They are not afraid to take a hard look at their own work and find ways to improve it. They also are not afraid to open their minds to fresh ideas about old topics. This is the story of what we learned.

IDENTIFY STUDENTS' NEEDS

Chilly November air seeped through a slightly opened window of Marilyn Lopez's fourth-grade classroom at P.S. 206 in Queens. I sat watching two students huddled together on the rug. Melissa was reading aloud to Carrie, pointing her finger at each word in the text. While she read without much struggle, Melissa gave each word equal time and value. She moved from word to word with the same tone of voice and rhythm. Carrie yawned. I wondered, was it a yawn of comfort and contentment in the sharing of a book? Or was it, more likely, boredom?

"Girls, I need to talk to you," I said, settling across from them on the rug. "Tell me how your reading is going."

"Okay," they answered together, predictably.

"I noticed something about you when I was sitting over there," I said. "I noticed that one of you yawned."

Carrie blushed. "Yeah."

"Tell me more about that yawn."

I could see by her shrinking shoulders that Carrie was embarrassed about the reason for her yawn. She knew her partner's reading was, well, monotonous.

"This isn't a boring book, is it?" I asked.

"Oh, no," Carrie answered. "I love Amber Brown."

I pulled closer to them. "Melissa, do you love Amber Brown, too?" I asked Carrie's partner.

She smiled. "Yeah. She's funny."

"Did it sound funny when you were reading it?"

Melissa shook her head.

"Well, I was watching you read, Melissa, and I noticed something. I noticed that although you were getting all the words, you weren't getting all the punctuation. In fact, you were reading right through it. Sometimes it seemed as if there wasn't any punctuation there at all."

Melissa frowned and glanced at the page. "Um, I didn't think of that."

"Here, let me show you something. I'll read the same page you just read, but I'll use the punctuation marks as road signs to help me read."

I read only part of the paragraph when Melissa interrupted me. "That's the same story?"

"Same story, same words." I showed her the book. "You need to use the punctuation to help you read, Melissa. What I want you to do is to go back and reread some of this book and to rehearse your reading. Take a few lines and read them over and over, but especially use the punctuation to show you where to pause or stop or change your voice. Do that for a while and see how it helps you read more like an actor saying her lines. And ask Carrie to coach you."

I knew I had to check up on Melissa and Carrie soon, because I wasn't sure what they knew about how punctuation changes the way one reads. But I was glad that now they at least knew to use their voices fluidly to create meaning.

Perhaps you find this happening occasionally among even the so-called proficient readers in your room. Children may read right through the punctuation on the page as if it weren't there. Often they seem to not notice periods or commas, nor do they adjust their voices to the ups and downs of normal speech that punctuation helps us recreate. If written language is largely spoken language transferred to the page by symbols, then reading the symbols should help the reader recreate the writer's voice. As I said before, some children are so intent on getting the words right that they don't see those small dots and lines.

This is true in writing, too. Children are often so intent on getting the words down that they lose the wonderful and necessary rhythm that punctuation creates. By foregoing an important tool to get their meaning across, they miss the opportunity to shape their audience's reading of their work.

ASK THE TOUGH QUESTIONS

I discussed this issue with a group of teachers, including Aliza Konig from P.S. 165 in Manhattan. Aliza wanted to do a punctuation study, but she was concerned that her students wouldn't retain what they learned. She feared the exciting things they might discover about punctuation would be lost if she didn't return to them again and again. But she also feared that repetitive drill would sap their enthusiasm.

"How do we keep it at the front of their minds?" she asked. "How do we keep it fresh and new, but make it second nature as well?"

These questions seem to sum up many of the dilemmas we face as teachers. We want our students to retain fresh minds for learning, but we know some information risks becoming stale even as it becomes part of their repertoire.

KEEP THE PUNCTUATION ENERGY FLOWING

Aliza's questions often plague us. In the comfort of "I've heard this before" is also the danger of dismissing something important, and we know children often turn us off when they think they "already know it." In addition, we remember only what we use. Think of how hard it is, for example, to retain a foreign language if you don't speak it regularly. And the truth is punctuation is a "langue" students may not "speak" every day. They often use it only when we insist on it.

There is a big difference between knowing about something and being able to do it well—for example, between reading the driver's manual and getting behind the wheel, between passing the road test and getting thousands of miles of experience driving in all kinds of weather. When you practice, you can't help but get better. You refine your technique, you learn subtleties, as in driving around curves at night. Deepening and refining knowledge is one way to keep the energy flowing. It's also one way to master a skill so it becomes second nature. The next sections cover some daily things we can do to make sure that our teaching about punctuation sticks.

What Must Happen in Classrooms for Students to Learn Punctuation

HAVE STUDENTS READ A LOT EVERY DAY

To become and remain familiar with punctuation, children must read authentic texts every day. I know that, for some of us, finding reading time seems like an enormous luxury. So many other legitimate, valuable school experiences pull at us, that it's not surprising so many of

---

For students to learn punctuation they must:

◆ read a lot every day

◆ write every day for a sustained amount of time

◆ receive direct instruction in written conventions

Ways to Weave Read-Aloud Activities Throughout the Day

◆ Read a poem in the morning.

◆ Read a picture book before lunch.

◆ Read from a chapter book on an ongoing basis, at a point in the day of your choice.

◆ Read a nonfiction selection as children collect their belongings to leave the room for a special. Short pieces from magazines such as *Muse* work well.

◆ Read an editorial as the children are packing for home.

◆ Refer back to read-aloud texts frequently during the day to make literature connections and teach writing strategies.

us complain of not having enough time to get it all in. Yet we can never expect children to become better readers if they do not read every day for a significant amount of time. (Krashen, 1993; Calkins, 2001). And that includes reading with punctuation awareness. Indeed, one of the many reasons I will never play for the NBA is because I do not devote enough time to shooting baskets every day!

Children who engage with text regularly are used to seeing punctuation. Good readers know what it feels like to understand what they read, and they know how to use everything on the page to build the story's world in their minds. They know how it feels when meaning breaks down, and they have strategies they can call on to help themselves. This is not to say that knowing about punctuation will solve all reading problems, because punctuation is only one piece of a complicated cognitive process. However, constant reading will help make students better readers who are more aware of the nuances of written language, among which is an author's use of punctuation.

Teachers need to read aloud to their students at least twice a day. Read poetry, nonfiction, new articles, chapter books, sports articles. Read, read, read. Read literature you love, and read it so they will love it, too. It's important to practice reading aloud beforehand, because few things are more boring that a dull read aloud.

The time invested in reading aloud is time well spent. Unfortunately, many children do not have the experience of being read to at home; these children will never have this experience if we don't provide it for them. And there is something special about sharing a book together. Even adults like to go to readings by authors to hear voices recreating the written word. As someone who spends hours commuting in my car, I am a fan of audiobooks. Someone is reading to me several hours a day. How lovely.

As for punctuation, reading aloud gives students a sense of the cadence of language and of the way they should sound when they read a book. Stopping and pausing or slowing down at certain points are subtleties children learn only if we model them. As they sit listening, children pick up more than just plot and character. They are learning how a book sounds and how they might want their own writing to sound.

The problem is that there is so much else to do, especially as students move up the grades. Some teachers, administrators, and parents mistakenly believe that older children do not need to be read to because they can read to themselves. They believe that reading aloud is wasting time. I ask that those adults read some of the books available on the topic. (See box at right.) In the meantime, do all you can to let your students hear wonderful books.

HAVE STUDENTS WRITE EVERY DAY FOR A SUSTAINED AMOUNT OF TIME

Students cannot become facile at writing in general and using conventions in particular if they only do them now and then—no more than I can get thin by dieting on Fridays.

Books for Advice on Reading Aloud

- *The Read Aloud Handbook*, Fifth Edition, by Jim Trelease (Penguin)

- *Reading Magic: Why Reading Aloud to Our Children Will Change Their Lives Forever* by Mem Fox (Harvest)

- *Lasting Impressions: Weaving Literature into the Writing Workshop* by Shelley Harwayne (Heinemann)

Writing must happen every day. Not twice a week. Not eliminated because there's an assembly. Not after lunch to "calm them down." In order to get in shape, I must exercise, take vitamins, count calories. Eating right must become a way of life, just as writing accurately must become a way of life. It must happen regularly. Every day. Period.

Writing every day also means writing for a substantial chunk of time every day. Five minutes sandwiched between lunch and math will not give students the experience they need to become fluent writers. Try to set aside a minimum of thirty minutes a day, preferably more, for uninterrupted writing.

Along with writing every day comes the importance of making writing public. Students need to bring their writing to completion. They need to hone their skills on many pieces, in many different genres. They need to make plans for their independent writing lives: writing letters to grandparents, lyrics for songs, skits for shows, and whatever else represents the real world of writing. When writers put their work out for others to see, they sense that they're learning these skills "for a reason." It's the reason most music-educators require recitals; they know student musicians must work toward a performance. Publication is the student writer's performance.

Be aware, though, that when students spend too much time on one project, they tend to lose interest. How many times can they revise the same piece without getting tired of it, especially when they know so little about revising? But, once you have taught them many revision strategies, including use of punctuation, they can go back and revise with wisdom and with a sense of knowing much more than they did before. Requiring students to publish frequently gives them a folder full of drafts to work on, rather than one or two pieces they have beaten to death.

BUILDING STAMINA FOR WRITING

If you expect students to write for long stretches, you must help them build stamina. One way to do that is by teaching them to fill up their pages, to write a lot. Isoke Nia says she wants students to write long: long on the page and for a long time. (See box opposite.)

Most students are used to writing as little as possible, especially when they feel they are writing for the teacher rather than writing because they have something to say. We've all heard children ask, "Is this enough?" or my other favorite question, "How long does it have to be?" The answer is that it has to be as long as it should be, as long as it takes to tell a story with detail and clarity and suspense and all the other qualities of good writing. Most writers can't do that in three lines—which is why we are not all William Carlos Williams. So we must practice writing a lot on the page. And the more children write, the better their punctuation will get, because they will have more chance to practice it.

WRITING FOR A REAL AUDIENCE

When students believe that their teachers are their only audience, they tend to lose heart. "All this work only for a grade?" is what some of them think. But when students know that their work will make its way through the school and even into the community, they are more likely to work hard. When they know that the third-grade class down the hall, for example, will be getting their papers to read and might be writing back to them with comments, there is more at stake. When they

---

Strategies for Getting Students to Write More

◆ Write to a mark placed appropriately far down on the page.

◆ Choose a phrase and write more about it. Stretch it out.

◆ Zoom in on a corner of your story and write more about it.

◆ Add dialogue or description.

◆ Slow down the action and tell it longer.

◆ Set a timer and keep your pen going.

◆ Add in the internal story. What was happening in your head or body? (For example, "My heart was racing.")

◆ See Lucy Calkins's *The Art of Teaching Writing* (Heinemann) for more ideas.

---

know that they will not be following their papers to the second-grade class to explain what they mean, they are more careful because their writing has to stand on its own. When their papers might be going to the local senior citizen center or firehouse, they become more invested. There is a sense of pride and honor in their work. The writer wants readers to understand what was written. Punctuation is a tool for helping the writer get the job done well, and publication raises the stakes for everyone.

Seeing their writing around the school and in the community hammers home the need for correct punctuation. And, if students are asked to comment on a paper that is not well punctuated, they will see first hand how difficult it is to read. Publishing goes both ways. It helps children see that, because writers write for real purposes and expect their work to be read and understood, it's important to be careful about conventions.

PRACTICING IN A WRITER'S NOTEBOOK

The best way for students to become skillful is to practice, and the best place for practice is in their own notebooks. Since notebook writing comes from students' own intentions, the notebook is a good place to "try out" the punctuation they have learned. It is also a good place for them to work on getting something right. So, for example, a writer might try the same sentence punctuated three different ways in a notebook before transferring it to a draft. I said earlier that punctuation should become a primary act of composition. For that to happen, children should be thinking, "What is the best way to punctuate this?" as they are composing. It is hard to do this "on the fly," but children who use their notebooks as workbenches for solving writing problems learn to see this as a natural way to work.

Occasionally we need to have children try out a particular use for punctuation, for example, using commas in dialogue. Exercises such as these should be done with the child's own writing, probably with writing already in the notebook. After talking about ways to use commas, ask children to practice in their notebooks, where they should have lots of their own writing. Because the writing is their own, the purpose of using commas—to clarify meaning—will most likely make more sense.

I am not an advocate of worksheets that provide "practice" in using punctuation. At best, these activities gesture at punctuation practice, but never get to the heart of why punctuation is important (i.e. to help authors convey their inten-

Suggestions for Making Writing Public

◆ Bind the class work in a simple book and add it to a school or classroom library.

◆ Share papers with at least two other classes, with requests for comments. You may want to attach preprinted comment sheets. (See Appendix B, page 139.)

◆ Invite another class in for an informal reading. Have students share whole pieces at their tables or only a couple of lines as a class.

◆ Send the papers to an administrator or staff worker, including secretaries and maintenance people, who may be willing to read and respond to up to five papers, but not everyone's!

◆ Submit papers to the local public library for display. For example, send poems during April to celebrate National Poetry Month.

◆ Ask parents to read several papers and respond on a comment sheet.

◆ Host a class reading in the evening for parents, community members, and peers.

◆ Post excerpts from recent writing on a display board in the hallway or outside the school building.

tions). The truth of the matter is that we cannot punctuate someone else's writing with integrity, because we can't be sure how he or she wanted it to sound. Additionally, these worksheets are often repetitive and describe scenarios or use language that does not match a young person's experience. It is more meaningful— and wastes less paper—if we ask children to practice in their own notebooks.

Stuart works on punctuation in his writer's notebook.

> Stuart
>
> One day in my after school I whent to six flags with Dennis my brother and my mom! we tuck two buses to get to six flags. I was in my brothe's team and Dennis to the frist ride we got on was the water slide. I was crying when it whent up but when it whent down I stop crying. and I got wet. the second ride was the trane it whent fast but not very fast. it spined and spined after it was time to get off the ride. And the last ride was a worm ride. it was fun we screamed and moved we tuck 10 rides in the worm ride. And when I got out of the ride I smiled.

MODELING WHAT GOOD WRITERS DO

As a writing teacher, I often write along with my students. When I stop to think about whether I want to end a sentence with a period or join it to the next one with a comma and a conjunction, I am exercising a "right" as a writer. I want students to see that sometimes there are choices to be made, so I model my thinking in front of them. I show them the different ways the punctuation could go. I might even consult a style manual to demonstrate that I'm not only trying to be precise, but also to get just the right sound to the sentence.

Do not hesitate to do this, even if you are "not a writer." So much the better! If your writing seems to come too easily, you might discourage the children. Let them see you work at it, so they know that even adults sometimes struggle to get things right. I often worry that, in our efforts to make school "fun," we rob children of the joy of working hard at something and seeing the tangible results of that labor. Yes, writing is often hard work, but it is satisfying, too. Let them see you working hard at it and they will be more apt to give it a try.

EXPLORING WHAT PUBLISHED WRITERS DO

Look closely at the work of published writers, too, but resist revising it with the class. Instead, discuss why you think the writer made certain choices. For example, it seems inappropriate to change choices of E.B. White or Margaret Wise Brown.

Some Third Graders' Discoveries About Commas

◆ In a series of three or more items joined by a single conjunction, separate each one by a comma. **Kid language:** "Commas go in the spaces between any things in a list."

◆ Enclose parenthetic expressions between commas. **Kid language:** "Commas are like your hand beside your mouth when you are whispering an aside or extra information."

◆ Place a comma before a conjunction introducing an independent clause. **Kid language:** "If you put two small sentences together with words like 'and,' 'but,' or 'because,' you need a comma to hold the spot where you joined them."

◆ Do not break sentences in two. **Kid language:** "Don't let periods do a comma's work."

On the other hand, writers study other writers, just as artists learn from other artists and baseball players learn from other baseball players. Mentor writers can teach us miles of information if we just look to them (Ray, 1999; Flynn and McPhillips, 2000). Of course, it would be marvelous to have a writer-in-residence in every classroom, but in the real world of schools, this is highly unlikely. The next best thing is to show children how to study literature to learn what writers do, much the way we would study scores if we wanted to learn to compose music.

Learning to write from writers helps in all aspects of writing and should be at the heart of any punctuation study. When children see punctuation as something writers really use, and how choices writers make actually affect the way a story is told, the importance of conventions makes more sense to them. As they write more and more every day and begin to see themselves as writers, they see that punctuation can help them tell their stories.

Spend some time finding books you love by writers who tell wonderful stories and use punctuation to enhance the telling. I do not mean stories where the writer goes for the cheap shot and uses fifteen exclamation marks in a row to show excitement, because that is not what you want your students to do. Look for writing where the writer has thoughtfully, carefully, and artistically used punctuation. Study Jane Yolen's use of a comma, for example, as a composer might study Mozart's use of a rest. There is much we can learn from the experts in the field, and there are many secrets such study can reveal.

I have included a list of some of my favorite books at the end of this book, although the list changes frequently and grows every year. Sitting on the floor in the bookstore or public library surrounded by new and old children's books has become customary for me. While some may regard me as odd, I happily continue to find and horde the books I love.

Not every book I love represents wonderful use of punctuation, but most do. Most writers use every tool they can to tell their stories well. As teachers of writers, we can no more ignore punctuation and the experts in the field than composers can ignore a time signature. Our students and we have everything to learn.

GIVE STUDENTS DIRECT INSTRUCTION IN WRITTEN CONVENTIONS

We cannot assume that students who come to us in September know about punctuation. I have no doubt that their previous teachers have taught punctuation, but, as we've seen, that doesn't mean that children have learned it.

After assessing student understanding early in the year through observation, writing samples, and conferences, you should plan at least one early punctuation study. Even if your students appear to be using simple punctuation, it's important to push them toward more sophisticated usage soon into the school year. (See Chapter Two for a sample first unit of study.) If some of your students come from classes where punctuation was taught effectively, you might be able to move quickly toward advanced studies with them, while providing review for other students. (See Chapter Seven for examples of advanced studies.)

It's important to remember that the extent to which we use punctuation correctly, like all conventions, is often used to evaluate our intelligence. As teachers, we dream of opening opportunities for every child in our society, and to avoid allowing something as small but significant as punctuation to prevent those opportunities. The truth is that reading and writing have political and social significance in our society. (Bomer and Bomer, 2001).

To help open up these opportunities, each of the units of study in this book represents an inquiry into learning about punctuation. Teachers need to provide direct instruction in written conventions, but that instruction should be part of a sustained, larger inquiry (Nia, 1999). Random lessons that pop up here and there do not make as much sense to children, because the lessons have no context. A study over several weeks, or a string of mini-lesson over several days, helps children settle into new learning and create a mental picture to place it on.

We also don't want to confuse "mentioning" with teaching. Modeling by writing in front of a class, examining writing together, and looking at samples of children's writing is very different from just telling students something and expecting them to go off and do it. Study that is deep and wide accomplishes much more than reminders and nagging ever can.

Since I want to open up the full range of punctuation possibilities to students, and show my respect for them as writers, I allow them to investigate many ways to use each punctuation mark. We all have our favorite rules for, say, comma usage, usually because those were the ones we were taught in school. But commas have so much more potential. Students who use commas in myriad ways tend to be more effective writers. Once again, I emphasize that correct punctuation does not make for good writing, but is part of the total package.

Before You Embark on Punctuation Study. . .

For us to teach our best, we must continually study what we are teaching. After I decided to teach punctuation, I became fascinated by it. I read everything I could get my hands on about it, some of which was rather pompous and dry. Despite that, I realized how much fun punctuation could be, because I read widely and began to think deeply about the punctuation in the books I was reading. This kind of reading and thinking is important in making sure your knowledge is current and clear. It can also help you see the possibilities for fun in punctuation.

The Importance of
High Expectations

*I*n most of life, we are held accountable for what we do. If we take on
telephone service, we are responsible for paying the bill on time. If we get a
driver's license, we are expected to know and abide by the rules of the road. If
we become parents, we must provide certain basics for our children. And, while
written conventions are not a matter of life and death, being held accountable for
what they have been taught only prepares students for what will come later in life.

So why are we often afraid to insist that children use conventions correctly
after we have taught them? I agree that, until a unit of study is complete, we can
be somewhat flexible. But, once you have spent three to four weeks teaching something, doesn't it make sense to hold it up as a standard? We wouldn't think of
letting go of addition or subtraction once they have been taught; we agree that
math errors must be corrected and we push students toward accuracy. Why, then,
do we not hand back to a child the paper that shows a lack of concern for conventions, a lack of respect for the reader? I am not talking about occasional errors—we
are dealing with children, after all, who are, for the most part, doing their best to
master new and difficult material. But, in my opinion, it is not unreasonable to
calmly and gently refuse to read final papers that show complete inattention to
punctuation. (One exception is the work of children with special needs. Read
Individual Education Profiles carefully to know what is appropriate in each case.)

Rubrics are useful. There are many samples you can borrow from professional
books. I prefer to construct rubrics with the class, keeping in mind the teaching
that went on in that class. Some teachers give separate grades for content and for
conventions. I worry about the message that sends; children might misunderstand,
thinking that it's okay to forget conventions as long as your ideas are good. The
truth is that, no matter how good one's ideas are, no one will take them seriously
if the writer doesn't take conventions seriously. I would not want to listen to a violinist whose ideas about interpreting Mozart are brilliant, but who gets every other
note wrong. Ouch!

Therefore, let the children know that, while there is room for play and experimentation in notebooks and drafts, final papers ready for publication must be carefully edited. Once students know a lot about punctuation, this should not be a chore. They will already have done much of the punctuation thinking during composing and revision. Ideally, just before publication, they should need only to proofread.

Organizing a Year of Study

We want students to have many chances to become expert punctuation users, so the initial unit of study, a large block of time when punctuation is our major focus across all kinds of writing, takes place early in the year, in October or early November. (See Chapter Two.) It is followed by at least one other deep study of punctuation later in the year.

I suggest spending September setting up reading and writing workshop structures in your classrooms. (See Calkins, 1994, and Calkins, 2000.) Follow that with a unit of study in writing in a genre, such as personal narrative or editorial. Once students have produced pieces of writing from self-generated topics, it will be easier for them to see the importance of punctuation, because they will be invested in the writing. Your punctuation unit will be more powerful because children will see punctuation as a tool writers use to help them clarify what they want to say, and that readers use punctuation, again as a tool, to help them shape meaning during the transaction between themselves and the text (Rosenblatt, 1978). I also hold off until after September because I want students to understand that written conventions are not the only things that matter in writing. "What do I want to say?" is a question writers ask themselves, which really means: "What words will I use?" "How will I arrange them?" "How do I want my reader to read them?" The last question is why children must study punctuation.

Once students have settled into school and published at least twice, they are ready for the punctuation unit. By mid-October, they should begin to understand that the total package matters. I want to get lots of mileage from the initial unit by having students practice all year the topics we cover in that unit. Based on my assessment of how they are doing, I plan times to circle back to the punctuation unit to review or rediscover. I also want students to have maximum punctuation practice before spring testing, without needing to force-feed them test preparation for months.

Plan for a Year of Study in Punctuation: *Units Across the Year*

Time of Year	Type of Study	Duration of Study
Mid-October/ November	First Unit of Study	2–3 weeks
January/February	Follow-Up Unit of Study (examples: study within genre, of an author, of a specific mark)	2 weeks
March/April (test time)	**Review** (using punctuation in formal ways)	2 weeks
June	**Advanced Study** (grows from student interests)	2–3 weeks

By setting aside up to three weeks for each study, we have created a structure where nearly 10 weeks—one fourth of the school year—are devoted to some kind of punctuation study. Surely there will be returns on your investment when so much time is spent growing your students' knowledge base.

CHAPTER 2

Starting With What Students Know and Notice

A First Unit of Study in Punctuation

"Kid watching," as suggested by educator Yetta Goodman (1978), is a way to gather the information we need in order to know what to teach. So, during the weeks when I was studying ways to teach punctuation, I spent much of my time watching children to see what they do as they read and write.

Being a teacher-researcher is fascinating and empowering because it requires us to use our creativity and professionalism simultaneously. It also shows that no teacher guidebook can tell us what we need to know about the individual learners, because students (and teachers) are, by definition, individuals. We must watch our students and do the exciting work of figuring out how to teach them what they need to know. In addition, the information we gather from watching children with a particular angle in mind—for example, how they use punctuation to make meaning when they read—can lead us to uncover important information about how they approach any learning task.

Janet conducts
a mini-lesson on
how authors use
punctuation in
their books.

During my initial time of watching how children learn to use punctuation, it became increasingly obvious to me that many were not writing with punctuation because they were not reading with punctuation. Time and again I observed children reading without noticing what the periods or commas were telling them.

Whole-Class Work
Students Talk About What They Notice

Most process-oriented classrooms have a meeting area, often with a rug and several nooks and crannies where students can go to read undisturbed. So Lisa Duffy and I started by asking her students to sit with a partner in a comfortable place. We gave each pair of students a big book and asked them to read it together, looking at the "little marks" on each page and talking with one another about what they noticed about them. We cautioned students not to focus on the story—odd for a reading lesson—but on the range of dots and dashes, and to think about why the authors might have used them.

Guidelines for Listening In

◆ Give pairs of students big books to explore punctuation together.

◆ Ask students to talk about what they notice as they read.

◆ Listen carefully to what students say to each other, to gather information about what they know and what they are noticing.

◆ Use your notes to assess children's knowledge base.

◆ Begin to point children toward the writer's intentions by asking them to think about what the writer might have been asking them to do as readers.

◆ Chart their observations.

◆ Ask children to begin noticing punctuation in their independent books.

The ways students typically respond to this exercise are interesting. Some children appear to notice punctuation for the first time because it is so physically big in a big book. Others aren't quite sure what the punctuation is for—which is telling in itself—and merely count the number of periods. Some begin to look at the variety of marks, and, although they may have no names for them yet, remark that they see "a half circle with a period on its head" (i.e. a semicolon). Some notice marks that are familiar and are satisfied that they know what the marks mean: "The little open mouths before and after a sentence tell you that someone is talking" (i.e. quotation marks). With few exceptions, children are amazed and interested. For once, they are being asked to look at something besides the words to see how writers make the words work together to create meaning. We have opened their eyes to a new world, a world of nuance and shade. And, because we believe in inquiry, we are asking them to "figure it out," rather than telling them the answers or giving them the rules.

NOTICING HOW AUTHORS
USE PUNCTUATION

1. READ ALOUD A PASSAGE FROM A WELL-KNOWN BOOK

Lisa feels her students already have some knowledge of punctuation marks, so she begins her first punctuation mini-lesson by reading aloud the first page of a book the class already knows well, *Owl Moon* by Jane Yolen. Earlier, Lisa wrote the text on a chart:

> **It was late one winter night, long past my bedtime, when Pa
> and I went owling.**

As she reads it aloud, she points out that the commas in the middle of the sentences make her voice do something. Most students notice the short pauses that the commas signal.

2. HAVE STUDENTS WORK IN PAIRS

Lisa asks her students to turn to their partners and talk about how the meaning might change or be confusing if the pauses weren't there. She and I then listen in on one or two groups. We hear students say things such as "The beat of the sentence would be different" and "You'd think her words were all jumbled up." One child says that he heard no difference, so his partner proceeds to read the sentence aloud to him one word at a time emphasizing the pauses.

Other children notice sophisticated things. For example, Jennifer says, "I think that if that first comma wasn't there, she'd have to use the word 'and.' But then the rhythm of the sentence would be changed. Like singing a song all wrong."

"Yeah," Jeremy says. "Or you'd think it was just a too long sentence and you could trip reading over the words."

"I don't think I would understand it if she didn't make me slow down with the commas," Eric says.

"I think you have to read that sentence in three parts," adds Kenesha. "And without the commas, you wouldn't have three parts at all, just a mess."

Already students are beginning to turn up their thinking about what punctuation does to reading. Lisa's mini-lesson showed them what she wanted them to learn by revisiting the text of a book they knew well. Looking at this text allows the children to study punctuation in the context of writing by an experienced practitioner, Jane Yolen, rather than trying to apply a list of external and potentially confusing rules to their own writing.

3. ENCOURAGE SMALL-GROUP INQUIRY WITH BIG BOOKS

We give small groups of students big books and have them read through the books together. Again, we ask them not to focus on plot, but to look, instead, for interesting punctuation and how it helps them "get" the meaning of phrases or sentences. We hear groups talking about how the reader knows the way the author wants the sentences to sound.

TRANSCRIPT OF A TYPICAL GROUP'S CONVERSATION:

Michael: Look, on every page there are these three dots (i.e. ellipses).

John: Periods.

Michael: No, they don't work like periods, 'cause these aren't sentences.

John: Maybe they're cutting off.

Michael: What?

John: Like someone is talking and someone else cuts them off.

Michael: Oh yeah. But there's no talking. See? No quotation marks.

John: I don't know.

Michael: Maybe it's one sentence that goes to the next page.

John: Yeah, maybe.

Michael: Yeah, look. It is.

John: So why three periods when it's the middle of the same sentence?

Michael: I don't know. Let's ask.

John: Could it be like the author is saying, "Get ready for what's coming?"

Michael: You mean like coming attractions.

John: Yeah. Like that.

TRANSCRIPT OF A STRUGGLING GROUP'S CONVERSATION:

Susan: I don't get it.

Amy: We got to look at the dots.

Susan: What for?

Amy: I don't know.

Susan: (*shrugs*) I still don't get it.

Amy: Maybe we should ask.

Susan: (*shrugs*) What are they doing? (points to next group)

Amy: (*watches*) They got a different book.

Susan: All they're doing is talking about the wiggle marks.

Amy: So?

Susan: (*scoots closer to next group and watches them*) Look, Amy.
They're talking about how the dots are different. I mean that they
mean something different.

Amy: So now what?

Susan: We look in our book here. For the dots. (*flips through pages*)
Like this one here. Weird. What is it?

Amy: That's two of them together. One's on top of the other (i.e. a
colon). I wonder what that means.

Lisa and I rejoice! Despite the disparity in the sophistication of their talk, all students make headway into recognizing that punctuation aids in creating meaning. We conclude that students, for the most part, know what punctuation is, but don't understand its power. They have never been given the time to negotiate meaning using punctuation marks as clues, because they have never been taught to look at text this way.

4. Return to the Meeting Area for a Class Share

We call students together for a share and ask them to tell us what they discovered. Their findings are interesting, and some quite complex. A few children are still at the level of merely noticing that there were some dots on the page. That is okay; they are beginning to realize that there are different types of marks and that each one has some meaning, even if they haven't discovered it yet. Further, the class share opened a window for these students; they saw the value in noticing something and coming up with an idea about what the author was doing.

We gather students' findings on a chart listing the punctuation mark, the text in which it was found, and the reason the author may have used it. (See Appendix C, page 140.)

Punctuation

What we noticed	What it meant	Examples of work
Periods .	stop	A bird lived in an old tree.
Comma ,	stop, pause, and take a breath	Once upon a time, in a house in the woods
exclamation Mark !	To say something louder. It makes it more exciting	An apple a day!
quotation marks " "	Someone or something is saying something. We use quotation marks with dialogue	"cluck, cluck, cluck," said the hen.
ellipses...	stop and pause	He heard a voice say ...

A class charts an author's punctuation intentions.

APPLYING THE LESSON TO STUDENTS' OWN WORK

In the writing workshop, Lisa continues the line of thinking by asking students to look in their notebooks for writing in which they used punctuation in interesting ways. Many students had never, or hardly ever, used punctuation before, which, of course, we know. This exercise provides them with an opportunity to take a good look at their own habits. Some children revise old entries by adding punctuation. As with anything new, they tend to "overuse" punctuation, especially the more exciting marks. But we all like to use new things a lot. (When I got a new bread machine, I used it every day until the newness wore off.) So Lisa and I are confident that, say, the children who were using twelve colons on each page will eventually settle back into an appropriate number as they gain facility and experience with using them.

EXTENDING THE LESSON TO INDEPENDENT READING

The next day Lisa has students apply the thinking they had done with big books to their independent reading books. As they look back over parts they had read, she hears them reading sentences aloud, thinking about how the author wanted them to be read. The children conclude that the punctuation marks are the author's instructions on how to read his or her writing, "road signs" on the page. The idea of author's intent was born—and, as a result, students begin to think about how they want their own writing to be read.

MODELING AN AUTHOR'S INTENTIONS

The next time we meet as a class, I do some writing on the overhead projector, and ask the students to help me "play" with the punctuation to shape the meaning. I show them how I draw on my experience of how punctuation works to help my readers. I decide how I want the piece to sound, and then I think aloud about how the punctuation will help my readers "hear" that sound. I think aloud about the rhythm I want to achieve. I let students see me choose the punctuation, because I want them to see how it will serve the meaning and tell my readers how I want the piece to be read. (See next page for a transcript.)

I also think aloud about some of the accepted conventions of comma usage that help me make decisions, because I want students to know that decisions like that are not arbitrary. Many children recognize quickly that commas separate items in a series, so I begin by modeling that rule. Because children often don't notice that commas separate two independent clauses joined by a conjunction, that is one rule I really want to demonstrate to them.

At one point, I say I'm not sure how to punctuate the sentence. I need to look it up in *The Elements of Style*. I want students to know that even adult writers must sometimes look for guidance in style books. I plant the idea that there is a way of using punctuation that makes sense, melody and phrasing that exist beyond aimless play, and that there are places where writers can look up this information.

More Ways to Help Students "Discover" Punctuation

◆ Hold class discussions about what students discover about punctuation in their reading.

◆ Create a class chart of students' findings. Write entries in their own language.

◆ Include examples from books and add them to the chart.

◆ Use daily read aloud to build awareness of rhythms of words and shapes of sentences.

1. THINK ALOUD ABOUT PUNCTUATION

I put the following draft of a short-story beginning on the overhead.

Mama picks up games at garage sales if there are pieces missing we use pieces from other games sort of mix and match we have no complete sets only bits and chunks you can think youre playing clue and find out we beat you with monopoly rules tonight were playing risk which in our house can be pretty risky

Now Papa is laughing his big laugh he spreads the pieces out and gives us all our armies pink yellow blue green purple armies such a silly game for a family that hates disagreements let alone war but Papa is serious about game playing he whistles and winks and shuffles card and says hes in a winning mood and taking bets we bet him two ice cream cones that we can beat him

2. INTRODUCE THE PURPOSE OF THE LESSON

Teacher: "This is a draft of some writing I am working on. I'm going to work on the punctuation while you watch. I want you to know that in the real world, I would never have written this without punctuation. I did it just so I could show you what I'm thinking. Writers rarely write without punctuation and then go back to put it in. So let's just pretend I am trying to get my punctuation in this writing to help my reader read it."

3. USE A MARKER TO REVISE PUNCTUATION

Teacher: "Mama picks up games at garage sales" That sounds like the end of the sentence to me, so I'll put a period there. "if there are pieces missing we use pieces from other games sort of mix and match" I know I have to change the "I" to a capital in the word "if" because now it's the beginning of a sentence. And I want my reader to pause after "missing," so I'll put a comma there. I also want my reader to pause after "games," so I could put a comma there. Is there any other punctuation mark I could use to make it sound like this? (*I read the sentence with "sort of mix and match" as an afterthought.*)

Eddie: How about a dash between "games" and "sort?" It would slow the readers down more than a comma, the way your voice slowed down more than a comma.

Teacher: Good idea. I like that. And I think it's an acceptable use of a dash, so let's do it. (*I change my comma to a dash.*) The next meaning chunk seems to be "we have no complete sets only bits and chunks," so I'll change that "w" to a capital and put a period at the end.

Maritza: Wait. Don't you need a comma after sets? We kind of slow down there when we read it.

Teacher: Hmmm, I agree. I'll put that in. Now the next chunk has some things in it that I don't even have to think about, because they are spelling rules that don't depend on how the writing sounds. The word "youre" is two words smashed together, so I have to put in an apostrophe and write it "you're." That's just the way it's done. And I see the same thing again in the word "were." It's a contraction of "we are," not the word "were," so I have to put in the apostrophe to show I left some letters out. And "Clue" and "Monopoly" are the names of games, so they must have capitals.

The next place where I see I have to do some hard thinking is "he spreads the pieces out and gives all of us our armies pink yellow blue green purple armies." The "h" in "he" needs a capital. That's a spelling rule for sentence beginnings. But this part at the end, where I say a list of colors, could be confusing for my readers. This is how I want it to sound: (*I read it slowly and deliberately*). What do you think?

Eddie: That's easy. Just put commas in.

Sam: Commas won't slow us down enough. You should put semicolons.

Teacher: Sam, I think semicolons won't work there. Each part of the list isn't long enough.

Sam: So add in "and" between them. That will slow readers down.

Teacher: Like this? . . . "pink and yellow and blue and green and purple armies."?

Sam: Yeah.

Eddie: No, don't do that because you have a string of "ands" later on where it says "he whistles and winks and shuffles." I think you should use the commas.

Teacher: I think so, too. I often find that the conventional way is best, unless I'm trying for a special effect. I think the commas will slow readers down enough, but not grind their reading to a halt.

4. ENCOURAGE STUDENTS TO APPLY THE IDEAS IN THEIR OWN WRITING

Teacher: So, today when you are working on your writing, find a place where you can do this kind of careful thinking about punctuation. Mark it with a star or a highlighter, and we'll talk about it during our share time.

Small-Group Work
Researching Specific Punctuation Marks

*L*isa feels her students need more information about punctuation before they can make informed decisions. So the next step is for them to meet in small study groups, with each group researching one punctuation mark of its choice. As a whole class, the children identify the punctuation marks that they want to study in depth. For the most part, these are marks that they feel are odd or unusual, such as the semicolon, the colon, the dash, and the question mark. Each child signs up for a group by signing his or her name below the mark on chart paper. (See photo next page.) The lowly period has no fans at all, so we tell students we expect them to use the period regularly and correctly, since nobody deems it worthy of study.

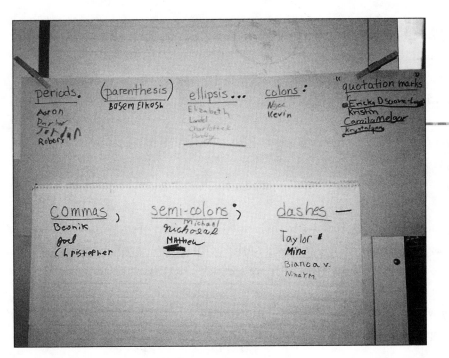

Students sign up for punctuation research.

The groups search through books in the classroom library to gather evidence on ways that authors used the mark they chose. Over the next two or three days, they compose definitions of the mark, with literature examples to support their theories on how writers use them to create meaning.

Students scatter around the room and spread books on the floor. We hear much negotiation and vigorous challenges among group members. We are excited that they do not just accept each other's descriptions passively. They construct their own understandings from authentic materials. Take this exchange, for example:

Jules: When you see three dots in a row it means, "Hold on. Something big is coming next."

Frances: Yeah, but sometimes those three dots can mean that the author left something out, or that somebody cut the speaker off.

Mary: It could also mean to slow down your reading and make your voice go lower and get stretched out. Like this . . . Boo!

Jules: I still like it when you have to get ready for what's next. I think

I saw some authors use that at chapter endings to make you keep reading.

Mary: Yeah, what's that called?

Jules: Hangers?

Frances: Cliffhangers!

Jules: (*laughs*) That's it. I'm going to go look for some in a book.

Mary: Me, too.

Frances: Don't forget we have to make a chart.

The group work takes students to their notebooks, where they think about their intentions. They play with the meaning of the writing by playing with the punctuation. Of course, we see some pages that are sprinkled heavily with semicolons and dashes, but we are confident that they will soon learn to use them sparingly, like black pepper.

Eventually, students return to the "How Authors Use Punctuation" chart and add a column of examples from their own writing. After all, they have begun to use punctuation with the same kind of intent as the authors they quote.

Mary uses punctuation to build tension in her writing.

FINDING PUNCTUATION IN THE REAL WORLD

Students can hear all we have to say about punctuation (or anything else for that matter), but, if there are no real-life connections, little will stick. So we ask them to form groups and to "go out into the world" to study punctuation. We brainstorm a list of places where they might find interesting punctuation in the world besides in books, and then we make an appointment to meet together in three days to talk about what they find. (See box at right.) There is much buzzing and laughter as they search for unusual, insightful, or blatantly incorrect or odd uses of punctuation in the world.

When we meet next, students have books, clippings from newspapers, and copies of advertisements. In small groups, they share what they had found. Then each group decides on one sample to bring to the entire class. They also try to determine if the text shows a typographical error, a clear mistake, or an example of craft (Ray, 1999). The conversations are often deep, interesting, and even comical. One group displays a paper placemat from a local diner as evidence of punctuation gone amok. The students feel smart to see how much they already know about punctuation.

Places to Look for Punctuation

- ◆ Newspapers
- ◆ Notes
- ◆ Magazine articles
- ◆ Letters
- ◆ Song lyrics
- ◆ Sports cards
- ◆ Billboard ads
- ◆ Event tickets
- ◆ Magazine ads
- ◆ Greeting cards
- ◆ Placemats
- ◆ Sale brochures
- ◆ Store posters
- ◆ E-mail
- ◆ Movie posters or ads
- ◆ Signs
- ◆ Direct-mail materials
- ◆ Yellow pages

The first unit of study convinced me that students need to know more about punctuation. They need the freedom of not being constrained by controlled texts or simplified versions of literature. They need teachers who are willing to reexamine their own ideas about punctuation, and possibly relinquish information they were taught in school that may not be accurate, but was school expedient. (For example, you may actually begin sentences with "and" or "but" as long as you avoid writing fragments.)

Students need to notice punctuation, talk about it, and play with it. Most of all, they need to discover it, not have it force-fed to them on worksheets or as rules to be memorized. They need to discover all the ways writers use the colon or semi-colon and the fun you can have with dashes. Suddenly, the comma is not a rule to recall; it's a way to shape your reader's understanding. This knowledge brings power to the little dots on the page, and power is, after all, what we want to teach children in their writing.

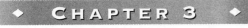

CHAPTER 3

Building on Students' Knowledge

Follow-Up Units of Study

B ased on the grade you teach and your observations of your students' needs, you will decide the follow-up unit of study. You may already have some ideas. But remember, our teaching should build students' capacity to work and use their knowledge independently. This means we must hold ourselves to a high standard. (Unfortunately, "because they love it" is just not a good enough reason to carry out an idea.) I avoid having kids dress up as commas and semi-colons, write letters to the quotation marks in a book, and edit published writing because I've found that ideas like that don't build independence. In this chapter, I share more effective ways of approaching punctuation.

Your Next Unit of Study

Let's assume you've done an initial punctuation unit of study. You have:

◆ assessed the student knowledge base in punctuation and planned instruction accordingly.

◆ given students opportunities to discover punctuation in authentic texts and to talk about it with peers.

◆ provided time for students to examine literature and discuss authors' intent in using punctuation.

◆ required students to try out punctuation choices in their own writing, using their notebooks as "workbenches" for practice.

◆ held students accountable for using punctuation in all their writing, including first drafts, while allowing for changes during revision and editing.

At this point, most of your students may be using punctuation regularly, though some may still be struggling. With this in mind, it's time for you to design a follow-up unit. While the purpose of the first unit was to make children aware of how punctuation creates a certain sound and rhythm in a text, a follow-up unit could focus on one of several topics, including:

◆ **an author:** an examination of the ways one author uses punctuation

◆ **a genre:** an examination of the ways punctuation is used in a particular genre, such as poetry or sports writing

◆ **a specific mark:** an examination of how one mark is used across genres. (In this study, the entire class typically looks at the same mark, rather than the small group inquiries described in Chapter Two.)

These topics could be the focus an advanced study later in the year, as well. The following is a detailed look at one such study.

Sample Unit

How One Author Uses Punctuation

CHOOSING AN AUTHOR

There are many authors of children's books whose work is worth studying on a variety of levels. Those authors may already be well represented in your classroom, and you can easily use their books as models for student writers. Or you may have books stored in your classroom library for children to consider for independent reading. The following study is based on the work of Cynthia Rylant, but it could easily be adapted to other authors. I encourage you to choose an author who uses punctuation in interesting and thoughtful ways, as a craft technique (Ray, 1999), as opposed to one who follows rules strictly and takes few risks. Such an author is acceptable, but the work will not provide as many opportunities for rich conversation and debate. In a punctuation study, it's important to discover new knowledge, not just hammer home the same knowledge students have.

Guidelines for Author Punctuation Study

- ◆ Choose an author who uses punctuation in interesting, thoughtful ways.

- ◆ Choose an author who writes in a variety of genres.

- ◆ Make the punctuation focus part of a larger study of the author's work, possibly in the last week, once students know the author well.

- ◆ Be sure to have many copies of the author's writing available for examination. (Librarians are usually willing to help if given enough notice.)

Because Cynthia Rylant writes in a variety of styles and genres, and many children like her, a study of her work can be very rich. Her picture books are particularly good as read-aloud selections, even in the upper grades. When using picture books with older students, I explain that I know the story is too babyish for them, but there are things to be learned about writing from it. Rylant is also prolific, so it is possible to fill your room with her books and have students studying multiple texts. Her vast number of titles also allows you to organize her work by genre and study punctuation across that genre (for example, punctuation in Rylant's picture books that sound like poetry). Assembling a collection of books should not be hard if you begin early. School and public librarians are usually willing to help if given enough notice.

Recommended Authors for a Punctuation Unit

Tomie dePaola

Mem Fox

Libba Moore Gray

Karen Hesse

Patricia MacLachlan

Gary Paulsen

Patricia Polacco

Cynthia Rylant

Jacqueline Woodsen

Jane Yolen

INVESTIGATING THE AUTHOR'S PURPOSE

I begin the week-long unit by reading aloud Rylant's simple picture book *Night in the Country*. (Any student who has studied with me has heard this book. It's a favorite.) In the discussion that follows, we return to a familiar landscape, reiterating some of the things noticed during our first study. Students feel successful being able to talk at length about the punctuation in this book and how it helps establish a rhythm and cadence. We return to the idea of author's purpose. The punctuation must serve the intent.

In Rylant's case, is seems her intent is to create a certain sound. For example, Marie Kupillas's second graders like how she often presents things in groups of three, such as " . . . in the fields, and by the river, and deep in the trees . . ." (Rylant, 1986). Pasha notices that this group is a list, and that commas separate each part of it. She listens for other places in the book where Rylant presents groups of three, and finds several.

Shima points out a place where Rylant uses a colon: "Listen: Pump!" Delighted by the onomatopoeic quality of that "Pump!," students want to know if Rylant uses the mark elsewhere. After examining a few examples, they theorize that one purpose of the colon is to signal your reader to pay special attention to what comes next. When they go off to experiment with using colons in their own writing, students make it clear to us that they understand one way writers use colons.

CHARTING STUDENTS' FINDINGS

That day, Marie begins a chart of specific ways Rylant uses punctuation in *Night in the Country*. She writes in the students' comments about the colon and the use of the commas in groups of three. Then we type out the text and make photocopies for students to study and to mark up in pairs. At the end of the next day, the students report back, and together we add their findings to the chart.

Interesting Ways Cynthia Rylant *Uses Punctuation in* Night in the Country

Punctuation Mark	Why Rylant Uses It	Quote from Book
Comma	To separate things in a list	"in the fields, and by the river, and deep in the trees"
Colon	Get ready for what's coming next	"Listen: Pump!"
Dashes	Here is some extra information for you	"while outside—in the fields, and by the river, and deep in the trees—there is only night"

CONFERRING WITH STUDENTS

By day three, the students are longing to look at some of Rylant's other work. So Marie lets them choose Rylant books from bins she has placed on each table. Children look through the books while Marie and I listen to their conversations and talk with some of the groups.

TRANSCRIPT OF GROUP CONFERENCE ABOUT RYLANT BOOKS:

Andre: Well, here in *Henry and Mudge* her punctuation is just regular.

Teacher: What do you mean by that?

Andre: Well, it's just regular periods and stuff. Or a question mark or exclamation mark. There's nothing fancy. She wants to keep it simple for the readers.

Teacher: Why would she do that?

Andre: Because she knows how hard we're working on getting the words, so she doesn't want to mess us up.

Diana: Yeah, but Andre, look at this. (*She shows a page from* An Angel for Solomon Singer.) She's got all sorts of stuff in here.

Teacher: What kind of "stuff"?

Diana: Well, look at this page. She uses those half-moons . . .

Andre: Parentheses?

Diana: Yeah, those, to tell us some extra stuff. It's not really part of the story, but it's nice to know. So we don't have to know that Solomon didn't have a fireplace before, but it helps us to get more of an idea about him.

Teacher: So why didn't she put it in without the parentheses?

Diana: Because then she'd be going back and forth between what's happening now and what happened to him a long time ago, and you could get mixed up about it.

Mamoud: It's like what she does with dashes in *Night in the Country*. You know that part that says, "while outside dash in the fields and by the river and deep in the trees dash there is only . . ."

Jose: I think she's also telling readers that she wants that part read quietly, like she's telling you a secret on the side. Like this. (*He reads* *the sentence and whispers the words in parentheses.)*

Andre: I wonder which reason is the real one.

Teacher: I don't think we could really find out.

Diana: We could write to her and ask.

Jose: Maybe she won't answer. Maybe she forgot.

Teacher: Well, I think you have some good hunches about why she used them. How could you test them out?

Diana: We could look at other parentheses in the book and see if that helps us to get better ideas.

Andre: Or if our ideas are good ones.

Jose: I still think she was trying to make it sound more like poetry, but in *Henry and Mudge*, she was making it easier for us to read.

Teacher: That's another hunch you could follow. You did lots of hard thinking today. Can you share that with the class?

WORKING IN SMALL GROUPS

On day four, the group goes off to look for parentheses in other Rylant books and compare her intentions with those in *An Angel for Solomon Singer*. Other groups find other things to study, such as how she uses commas to slow the reader down.

In small groups, students compare authors' use of parentheses.

By day five, the groups have arrived at some sophisticated ideas about why Rylant uses parentheses, semicolons, and other punctuation marks across several of her books, and they are ready to try the same things in their writing. It's important to remember that as children "play around" with punctuation, they attempt to do things that may be approximations of the "correct" way. If children have some space to practice and make mistakes, they will push themselves toward more conventional uses.

By the end of the study, students have a deeper sense of why Cynthia Rylant uses certain punctuation and how it contributes to her style. They begin to compare her work to other authors they are reading. Most important, they are better equipped to read like writers (Hansen, 2001; Ray, 1999) and keep their own readers in mind when they write.

Reading Like a Writer

Reading like a writer refers to going beyond the story itself to notice how the writer uses craft to achieve certain effects. When we ask children to notice how an author uses punctuation, for example, we are asking them to read like writers, to hone in on the techniques writers use. It is the equivalent of watching a baseball game like a baseball player versus watching like an average spectator. I see strikes and runs and errors, but a baseball player sees strategy and nuance and skill in holding a bat, which is beyond my scope or even interest. For more on this, see Jane Hansen's *When Writers Read* (Heinemann) and *Wondrous Words* by Katie Wood Ray (NCTE).

Sample Unit
Punctuation and Genre

It is interesting to think of the various genres children read and write in light of punctuation use. While I do not suggest this is the only lens through which to view genres, it can be a small part of a larger study—a window into better understanding of a particular genre. Examining, for example, the ways poets and sports writers use punctuation (often liberally) versus the ways essayists and textbook writers use it (more conventionally) can be powerful.

There are two ways to approach punctuation within a genre. The first is simpler and, therefore, more appropriate for students who are punctuation novices. The second is more sophisticated and could be done as a follow-up or advanced unit later in the year. (See Chapter Seven for detailed guidelines on carrying out both approaches.)

APPROACH #1:
STUDENTS LOOK AT A SPECIFIC GENRE

In this approach, students are working on a unit of study in a genre, such as editorials. Part of the unit is devoted to a week-long examination of punctuation, with discussions about ways editorial writers use it to help make a point. Some of their decisions may be determined by their personality; some of them by the topic the writer is examining. After reading editorials, making observations, and charting findings, much the same way they did in the author study, children return to their drafts and try out the punctuation techniques of the editorial writers they studied.

APPROACH #2:
STUDENTS LOOK ACROSS GENRES

Here students look across several genres to notice only the punctuation. The conversations that arise could revolve around comparisons of punctuation in, say, poetry versus chapter books or informational texts versus essays. These conversations can lead to observations about how writers of different genres use punctuation for different levels of freedom—for example, the poet has more latitude using punctuation than the document writer. What is the poet's intention versus the essay or report writer's? This study shows students how punctuation can help get the job done in a variety of ways, depending on the purpose of the job. Is the purpose to express grief or joy in a poem, for example, or to carry a reader along on a thought journey in an essay?

Good Professional Books for Teaching Poetry

- *For the Good of the Earth and the Sun: Teaching Poetry* by Georgia Heard (Heinemann)

- *Awakening the Heart: Exploring Poetry in Elementary and Middle School* by Georgia Heard (Heinemann)

- *A Note Slipped Under the Door: Teaching from the Poems We Love* by Nick Flynn and Shirley McPhillips (Stenhouse)

- *Wondrous Words: Writers and Writing in the Elementary Classroom* by Katie Wood Ray (NCTE)

- *Kids Poems: Teaching Students to Love Writing Poetry* by Regie Routman (Scholastic)

Here's an example of what such a study might look like. Let's assume the class has been working on poetry in a reading and writing workshop for about three weeks. The students have:

- read many poems in the classroom and outside.

- found two or three poems they really love.

- identified mentor poets from whom to learn.

- used their notebooks as resources for poem ideas.

- drafted some poems and done some revision.

There has been lots of talk in the room about poetry. It would be obvious to any visitor, from the talk and print in the room, that these children are deeply involved with poetry. All of this is important because the study of punctuation is embedded in a larger unit on poetry. The main focus of the unit is the genre, and punctuation is one piece of it.

Students might easily turn their attention to the punctuation in poems they already know well and love. If you anticipate shaping the poetry study this way, be sure some of the students' touchstone poems contain interesting uses of punctuation. Since everything about poetry is so deliberate, help children discover that, along with careful word choice and attention to rhythm, poets use punctuation to shape the way a reader reads a poem.

Conduct mini-lessons to show students how poets do that. Here are some ideas:

- Focus on the sound created by the punctuation and how it affects the aural reading of the poem (stops, pauses, hesitations).

- Demonstrate how to study punctuation by looking at your mentor poet's punctuation.

- Look at the precision and deliberateness of each mark and how it affects meaning.

- Rehearse a read aloud, attempting to get at the way the author wanted the poem read.

- Play around with punctuation in students' poems, and push them to use a wide variety of marks.

- Teach students to say why they made some of the punctuation choices they did, and how certain mentor poets informed their decisions.

Mentor and Touchstone Texts

Mentor texts refer to single books, poems, or an author's larger work that children, as individuals, decide to study. Therefore, it is possible for each child in the class to have a different mentor text or mentor author. A child might take on one book by Patricia MacLachlan as a mentor text or might study all of MacLachlan's work as a mentor author.

Touchstone texts refer to classwide texts that are used again and again in the classroom by the teacher and students for whole-group conversation and instruction. There are usually only two or three touchstone texts in each genre for a class. They are loved and known by all and help create a common conversation.

The two units of study on punctuation (the introductory study and the follow-up study) make the students' writing more precise and correct. The children understand that deep study and practice are essential to learning anything well. And the teachers who follow the work closely learn that merely perfunctory teaching of conventions only sends the message that punctuation is of small importance. When they are given the real-world tools of writers, children enjoy creating writing that makes sense.

CHAPTER 4

"Hearing" Punctuation

Read Aloud and Other Oral Reading Activities

Leslie Feldman, a fourth-grade teacher at P.S. 21 in Queens, is planning to move to literature-based reading instruction soon. She is busy leveling her library by studying her students and listening to them read to determine which books to steer them toward (Calkins, 2001; Fountas and Pinnell, 1996). She calls me over to sit with her as she listens to Matthew. "Reading is a chore for him," she warns. "But he works hard at it. I'm not sure how to help him."

As we pull our chairs close, Matthew looks up nervously from the literature anthology Leslie is using. His furrowed brow and pursed lips show how hard he is working. Leslie asks him to read aloud to us for a few sentences. Word by word, Matthew proceeds, laboring at sounding out every word. Clearly the selection is too hard for him and he is deriving no enjoyment, much less understanding, from the exercise. And just as obvious, the punctuation is not helping him. The dots on the page are causing overload, rather than smoothing and shaping the words for him. Matthew needs to be reading a simpler text that he can understand.

Often struggling readers work so hard to "get the words," they can't construct meaning. And, just as often, they don't use punctuation to help them. Again I am reminded of taking piano lessons as a child and spending all my energy getting the notes right. I had no energy left for the timing, which would have made my pitiful efforts sound like music. Similarly, so many children miss the music of reading, and, with it, the enjoyment and the meaning.

Many students do not understand that written words are meant to be reproduced in a spoken voice or a voice in their heads. So, one of the most powerful things we can do is read aloud to children, because it gives them a sense of the way texts should sound. We model for them how we, as experienced readers, use our voices when we read. Sometimes we might read directly from a book; at other times we might put a page from a book on the overhead and rehearse reading it in front.

May 17,

One golden, gorgeous glowing day... I went in the black car with my family. It was black like a night when there is no moon, star and electricity with dark cloud covering the sky. We drove on the high way and I was looking at everything that we passed. I was going to my dads friends house in New Jersey. I waited and waited and waited — until... I couldend stand it. Finily at last I am there I said. I took a deep breath of fresh air. It was a long time to get there it was long as sailing across the pacific ocean.

A student uses punctuation to reproduce the rhythm of speaking.

No matter how we do it, reading aloud has many benefits for children. Modeling our reading voices and, in the process, translating punctuation to voice are valuable activities. This chapter shows you ways to do that.

Favorite Read-Aloud Books for Noticing Punctuation

- *Between Earth and Sky* by Joseph Bruchac (Voyager)

- *The Quiltmaker's Gift* by Jeff Brumbeau (Pfeifer-Hamilton)

- *A Day's Work* by Eve Bunting (Houghton Mifflin)

- *Going Home* by Eve Bunting (HarperTrophy)

- *Twilight Comes Twice* by Ralph Fletcher (Houghton Mifflin)

- *Night Noises* by Mem Fox (Harcourt Brace)

- *My Mama Had a Dancing Heart* by Libba Moore Gray (Orchard Books)

- *Come on, Rain!* by Karen Hesse (Scholastic)

- *Night in the Country* by Cynthia Rylant (Macmillan)

- *Amos and Boris* by William Steig (Farrar, Straus and Giroux)

- *The Other Side* by Jacqueline Woodson (G.P. Putnam's Sons)

- *We Had a Picnic This Sunday Past* by Jacqueline Woodson (Hyperion Books)

- *Miz Berlin Walks* by Jane Yolen (Puffin)

DEMONSTRATING VOICE PATTERNS AND PUNCTUATION

Aliza Konig believes that looking carefully at punctuation surely helps her third graders. She has a strong read-aloud routine. She reads to her class several times a day, from a variety of genres. Sometimes the reading is for enjoyment, and sometimes it's for serious teaching—scaffolding students' thinking with the talk the reading creates, for example (Calkins, 2000; Wilhelm, 2001). She calls her class together in the meeting area and explains her plans about studying punctuation. She chooses to demonstrate her reading using Cynthia Rylant's *The Relatives Came*, a book the students know well.

1. INTRODUCE THE PURPOSE OF THE LESSON

Teacher: I've been noticing that, when some of you read, you don't use the punctuation marks to help you. One reason the punctuation marks are there is to help you know what to do with your voice. Some of you keep your voices flat like this . . . *(She repeats the same sentence in a monotone voice.)* But that's not the way we really talk and not the way we should read. After all, books are an author's way of talking to us, telling us a story, on the page. *(pause)* So what do you think about that?

Juan: Yeah, I do that flat thing.

Teacher: Why?

Juan: I don't know. I just do. I don't think about it.

Teacher: So maybe it would help you to spend some time practicing and paying attention to what your voices do, or should do, when you get to punctuation. You should remember that in November we did a unit of study on punctuation, and many of you studied commas.

Evelisse: We still have the chart we made hanging up over there.

Teacher: Yes. I hope you are looking at it when you need to and when you are writing. What I'd like you to do now is to study yourself as a reader. I'm going to give you the typed text of *The Relatives Came* by Cynthia Rylant, which you all know well. I'd like you to read the text to yourself and circle all the commas so you know where they are. Then I want you to read the text again and notice what your voice does, or what the voice in your head does, when you come to a comma. Jot down some notes in the margins about exactly what your voice does when you see a comma, and then we'll talk about it later.

2. HAVE STUDENTS WORK IN PAIRS

The children go off in partners. Aliza and I move around the room and listen to the students talking and reading to each other. There is lots of rereading, rehearsing, and note taking as students go back over sentences, trying to get them just right. We are delighted to discover that, when their attention is drawn to the

A student makes notes about how punctuation affects her reading voice.

voice element of punctuation, the children could read well. Aliza is seeing the read-aloud time paying off, as children emulate her reading voice. (See student sample, opposite.)

3. RETURN TO THE MEETING AREA FOR A CLASS SHARE

When we return to the meeting area, children share their notes. They recognize that a comma can "make you take a short breath," or "lower, then raise your voice." After this, we send them off to revise some of the writing in their notebooks by adding or deleting commas to give the same directions to their readers that the author gave to them.

Guidelines for Getting Students to Notice Their Reading Voices

- During your read-aloud time, ask children to pay attention to your voice and notice how it goes up and down. Provide time to process.

- Type up part of a well-known book and make photocopies.

- Distribute photocopies to the students, ask students to read them aloud in partners, and notice what they do with their voices. This works for "voices in their heads," too.

- Have students make notes in the margin about what they heard themselves doing with their voices.

- Post notes and provide time for students to talk about them in groups.

- Make a chart of student observations. (See sample next page.)

- Ask students to practice the exercise on a page in their independent reading books.

Class chart of how punctuation affects our reading voices

Punctuation

Mark	What it looks like	What it makes your voice do
comma	,	goes lower stops for a little bit - PAUSE
quotation marks	" "	sounds like the characters voice
period	.	stops lowers
exclamation mark	!	gets louder shows emotion (excited, angry)
question mark	?	gets higher
hyphen	—	pause continue
points of elipsis	. . .	goes up stretches
parentheses	( )	lowers
semicolon	;	like a comma - voice lowers pause

REPEATED READINGS AS PUNCTUATION PRACTICE

New teacher Heather Posnack was excited to see the punctuation reading work Aliza had done and wondered what it would yield for her fifth-grade class. She describes the process to her students as an actor doing a first, or cold, reading of a script. First, we demonstrate what we mean by showing a piece of my writing, with no punctuation, on the overhead projector:

> *The dogs are barking again causing a ruckus in the neighbor-hood and sending mrs beasley to the phone to call the cops on us and say that we don't control our animals and deserve a ticket and perhaps even a night in jail to think over how inconsiderate we are especially the dogs who will spend the night in jail with us so I call the dogs to come in and they run to me wagging their huge tails and I hug them and give them too many biscuits so they wont be worried about mrs beasley.*

The kids struggle to read it. Then we put up a copy of the same paragraph with punctuation. While it is easier to read, it is still challenging for many students. I read through it for them, telling them the decisions I made as a writer. I also talk about places where no decision was necessary, because conventional punctuation use dictated. (See Chapter Two.) In the end, we feel the students needed to practice reading aloud and hearing the punctuation.

So we ask them to find a page in their independent reading book that contains dialogue and narrative description, and to practice reading it aloud alone and then to a partner a few times. Audiotape recorders are useful here, because some children can't hear the difference in a reading until they hear themselves reading.

The students are surprised by how much their reading improves when they read the page repeatedly and become so familiar with it that they can focus on nuances of tone and voice. We even hear them asking partners, "Which way do you think sounds better?" The pacing created by commas, periods, and semicolons becomes important when they think of themselves as actors who are getting at meaning. Pretending to be actors also minimizes objections to reading the same page over and over. Heather asks them to do repeated readings once a day from then on— specifically, to find a page or passage and read it aloud a few times to a friend, sibling, parent, or pet. The important thing is to practice.

DICTATION AS PUNCTUATION PRACTICE

In her fourth-grade class, Marilyn Lopez has instituted a short dictation of two to four sentences every day. The sentences contain words she knows her students can spell, and some interesting, often complex punctuation.

Marilyn reads the sentences aloud, using measured stops but not exaggerating, while students write the sentences onto index cards. On their own, they check their sentences against a partner's, and then against Marilyn's version, posted on the white board. Students are free to

Sample Dictation:

Once, when I went to visit my grandmother, I saw three wild turkeys in her garden. What do people do when turkeys invade their gardens? My grandmother just shrugged. "They've got to eat, too, you know," she said to me.

challenge Marilyn's version. They can question her decisions about punctuation and offer reasons why they punctuated the sentences differently. Wonderful conversations happen when children negotiate to understand and verbalize their thinking.

Students who struggle with the dictation exercise, who have clear inaccuracies in their work, are put into a guided study group. Marilyn gives the group more practice and talks through the punctuation decisions writers make as they compose. Eventually, these students are writing or choosing sentences from books to dictate to each other, even doing their best to help (or trick!) each other. Their subsequent conversations show that real learning took place.

Guidelines for Doing Dictation

◆ Choose one or two sentences from books children know well. Include different genres, including humor. (You can also compose the sentences yourself, as Marilyn did.) Make sure all words are "spellable" so students can focus on punctuation.

◆ At a predictable time each day, gather students together, and have them bring pens and index cards or notebooks. Read a sentence in a natural voice, then ask students to write it down and share it with partners.

◆ On chart paper, white board, or the overhead projector, show the sentence as it appears in the book. Write it out before class so you don't waste class time doing it.

◆ Have students compare what they wrote with the original. Collect the children's versions to study. This will help you determine who needs additional instruction, who is right on target, and who is ready for advanced work. The emphasis should not be on whether they got it right or wrong, but on the decisions they made. So avoid grading and correcting their work. There is often more than one way to punctuate a sentence. We want to emphasize the thinking behind their choices, not whether they can think exactly like the author.

INDEPENDENT ORAL ACTIVITIES

Obviously, it is impossible for you to keep track of every oral comma and period heard in the room or every conversation and negotiation students have. But you can offer supports that help students move forward with little or no intervention. Here are some ways to do that:

◆ Provide tape recorders so students can record their punctuation rehearsal with or without partners.

◆ Audiotape your punctuation dictation. Place a tape player in a punctuation center, and expect all students to visit the center within a certain period of time. (See the next section for more on punctuation centers.)

◆ Ask students to listen to a short selection of a book-on-tape, recorded by someone other than you. The tape could be a professional recording, or one made by another teacher or an administrator. This is important because sometimes children are lulled by the sounds and patterns of a familiar voice. A fresh voice may provide new insights. It also may help students discern the nuances of speech from person to person. Be sure to provide a print version of the selection, too, so they can follow along to get practice in seeing and hearing the punctuation.

◆ Create a class audio-library. Have students record short selections of favorite poems or books. Student performers should give a brief introduction to the selection to establish a context and state why they chose the selection. This has further implications for literacy beyond punctuation awareness, since it invites wide and varied literary experiences and gives voice to the shy or quiet child. Make a class collection of these tapes, with the accompanying print.

◆ Ask students to read some of their own writing into a tape recording, providing a printed copy as well, so visitors to the center can follow along. Students can also point out on the tape a place where they used a punctuation mark deliberately, and direct the reader's attention to that place. For example, "In the third line I used an exclamation point, because I wanted you to know how surprised I was there."

• Incorporate music activities into the independent work. Clapping out the rhythm to a song, for example, is often done in music class. But it can also be used in language arts by asking students to clap out the rhythm of a sentence and think about how punctuation might help a writer or reader get that rhythm.

Center activities from Aliza Konig's fourth-grade classroom

Punctuation Centers

Commas, Commas, Commas!

Writers use commas for many different reasons. Read <u>An Angel for Solomon Singer,</u> by Cynthia Rylant. Underline with a colored pencil all the places you notice that have commas. Then, copy at least 2 different sentences you love with commas onto your "reading like writers" sheet, and fill in the other columns. Next, with same colored pencil, reread an entry in your notebook and put in commas appropriately. When you finish, you may work independently on your writing project.

Apostrophes

Writers use apostrophes for a couple of reasons. Reread Linda Sitea's story, <u>Zachary's Divorce</u>. Underline with a colored pencil all the places you notice that have apostrophes. Then, copy at least 2 different sentences you love with apostrophes onto your "reading like writers" sheet, and fill in the other columns. Next, with the same colored pencil, reread an entry in your notebook and put in apostrophes appropriately. When you finish, you may work independently on your writing project.

Parentheses

Writers use parentheses on purpose (they welcome the chance to use them). Read (or reread) <u>An Angel for Solomon Singer,</u> by Cynthia Rylant. Underline with a colored pencil all the places you notice that have parentheses. Then, copy at least 2 different sentences you love with parentheses onto your "reading like writers" sheet, and fill in the other columns. Next, with the same colored pencil, reread an entry in your notebook and put in parentheses on purpose. When you finish, you may work independently on your writing project.

PUNCTUATION CENTERS

Punctuation centers are a great way to give students access to information and opportunities to practice, while working independently or in a small group. Set up the center in a designated area of the room and either assign students times to visit it or ask them to sign up for a visit within a specified number of days.

Possible Center Activities

◆ If students want punctuation advice on a draft, have them leave a copy in a center "in box." Other students can proofread the draft or make comments on a stick-on note.

◆ Ask students to find examples of texts containing interesting punctuation use and place a copy in the center for others to see or for future discussion.

◆ Invite older students to listen to select parts of a song while reading the lyrics and think about the punctuation that the lyricist used or didn't use.

◆ Encourage students to punctuate the morning announcements. Specifically, record announcements as they are given over the PA in the morning, make a transcript, and have children punctuate it. Make the tape available in case they want to go back and hear the way the announcements actually sounded to ensure accuracy. Often the intricacies of spoken language can show children how vital punctuation is to understanding.

In the long run, I've found that children who learn to pay attention to punctuation in their reading not only become stronger readers, but also become more deliberate writers. Punctuation is one tool writers use to convey meaning, and, once they understand that, children enjoy reading aloud to each other. They also listen with more care when the teacher reads aloud.

CHAPTER 5

Conferring With Children

How It Informs Our Punctuation Mini-Lessons

I turn the doorknob quietly and tiptoe into Rob Ross's classroom at P.S. 206 in Rego Park, Queens. The students are sitting in a circle on the rug, listening to Rob read Louis Sachar's *Holes*, in a voice that reveals how much he is enjoying the book. Beyond the sound of Rob's voice, the room is silent—evidence that reading aloud is sacred here.

I watch the children. Some are looking at Rob, mouths open with expectation. Some are clearly listening, but gazing at the floor, the ceiling, their hands, pens, shoes. Diana is jotting notes on a stick-on note. Shinoa is doodling elaborate lace on paper. For some reason, Luis is making tally marks on a piece of paper.

Before he began reading, Rob had asked the students to listen to how Sachar reveals character. So, in the partner conversations that follow the reading, most of the children talk readily about things they heard. Here are some of the things they said:

Janet confers with students about an author's use of quotation marks.

- ◆ "Stanley uses some unusual words. Maybe he's too smart for his age."

- ◆ "Sachar makes us think Stanley is not a fighter because he just shuts up."

- ◆ "I think Stanley is confused because the chapter was confusing, you know, the writing was confusing."

- ◆ "Stanley is lame. How could he stand for all that injustice without fighting back?"

I draw close to Luis and Havel. Havel has just finished saying that Sachar makes him think Stanley is mysterious, because we don't understand a lot of what Stanley is talking about. And Luis responds with, "Sachar used 43 periods and at least 60 commas."

I stop myself from jumping right in, and I'm glad because Havel blinks and says, "What difference does that make?"

Luis just shrugs. But I could see where the teaching had gone wrong: Luis was confusing the purposes of read aloud and dictation. He believed that, during read aloud, he was supposed to listen for the number of punctuation marks he heard.

This is one reason why teaching can be so challenging. We teach lessons we think are right on target—and Rob's lessons are—but, very often, our students hear only part of what we say or misconstrue what we mean. When we ask "spot-check" questions, a few kids answer, and we assume that means the rest of them "get it," too. We ask if they all understand, and some nod and proceed to do either the wrong thing or nothing at all.

Watching Out for Students Who Need Help

Despite our best intentions and planning, sometimes there are Luises in our rooms, students who manage to slip by and carry misunderstandings with them for weeks or even months. How can we keep things from going wrong? How can we determine, early on, if kids are misunderstanding what we are trying to teach them? Certainly we can't know what every child is thinking at every moment. But we can practice one-on-one teaching, conferring, that gives us insight into individual students' learning.

In the definitive book on conferring, *How's It Going?* (Heinemann, 2000), Carl Anderson teaches us that what happens in a conference should be at the heart of our teaching. The best mini-lessons grow from our observations of children during careful, informed, and thoughtful conferences, as well as from the patterns that emerge from student writing and talking. Ideally, conferences inform our ideas for mini-lessons, and mini-lessons inform our conferences.

Rob had read *How's It Going?* and, therefore, knew the importance of taking notes on all his conferences. He had conferred twice with Luis during the punctuation unit, and, each time, had written about his serious doubts that Luis understood the work. Furthermore, Luis's writing showed a marked lack of attention to punctuation. No wonder Luis was counting periods. It certainly was creative of him, though, to think of something to do with punctuation, despite the fact he wasn't getting it and probably felt lost and lonely.

Although the punctuation study was over, Rob felt the need to support Luis and carry him along until he got it. By looking over his conferring notes, Rob identified two other students, Anna and Matesh, who also had shown a low level of competency. So Rob decided to do a small-group conference. While other children were writing during writing workshop, Rob called Luis, Anna, and Matesh together.

TRANSCRIPT OF A GROUP CONFERENCE WITH STRUGGLERS:

Teacher: I called you guys together because I'm concerned about how you are doing with punctuation. It seems that it's giving you lots of trouble in reading and in your writing. What do you think about that?

Luis: (*shrugs*) I don't know.

Matesh: Well, I have a hard time keeping it all straight in my head. Why don't they just put little stop signs if they want us to stop or little yellow lights to slow us down? It's really confusing.

Teacher: Can you say more about why it's confusing?

Matesh: Yeah, well, all the little marks have a bunch of meanings. How am I supposed to figure out which one the writer wants me to use?

Teacher: Luis, how do you feel about that?

Luis: (*shrugs*) I guess.

Teacher: So, what I'm hearing is that Matesh is confused about all the meanings that each of the little marks can have, and Luis sort of agrees with him. (*Both boys nod.*) And what about you, Anna?

Anna: I got so used to reading and not seeing the marks that I don't notice them anymore. I have a really hard time looking for them now, and it distracts me.

Teacher: Okay. What I think we need to do is work together to clear up some misunderstandings about punctuation. I think we should start slowly with our

Spotlight on Research

Frank Smith (1998) believes that learning should be effortless, continual, and independent of rewards and punishments. Learning that is part of social activity is never forgotten. He calls this "joining the literacy club." In fact, being part of "the club" helps a learner, because other members of the club help the learner say or understand what he or she wants to say. Not only do the other members of the club help us, but helping others helps us learn, ourselves.

Things to Remember in Punctuation Conferences

◆ Teach only one point per conference.

◆ Show the student what needs to be done, using literature or your writing.

◆ Do not make the changes for the student.

◆ Teach the writer, not the writing. Teach something that the student can apply to all writing from that day forward, not that applies only to the piece being discussed.

◆ Keep careful notes of what you teach each student, along with a plan to revisit that student, if necessary.

◆ Hold the student accountable for the teaching you did.

reading and just think of one page at a time until we get it right. (*Teacher takes out* Captain Underpants, *a simple chapter book most children find amusing*). I have three copies of this book. What I'd like you to do is to read each page to yourself and think about how the story sounds. Then, before you go on to the next page, I want you to read it to each other and talk about the way the reading sounds. Then slow down and look at the punctuation and actually say how the punctuation told you to read. Okay? You try that for a few minutes, and I'll be back to check how it's going.

What's good about this conference is that Rob figured out ways not only to support the children directly, but also to help them support each other, even though they had different problems. Also, he picked the right book. Leaning on high-interest literature such as *Captain Underpants* gets students to care about the story quickly. Naturally, if they like the book, they are more likely to work to try to figure out the many facets of the story. Rob was counting on *Captain Underpants* to give them the nudge to figure out the punctuation. And it worked.

Letting What We See Inform Our Teaching

*O*ften conferences reveal what our next mini-lessons, or group of mini-lessons, should be. Conferring early in the year can help you decide exactly when to do a punctuation unit. When we see ourselves as teacher-researchers, watching our students and shaping our teaching around observations, our teaching becomes sharp, focused, and precise. We also must accept the fact that the typical school year is approximately 180 days. And in those days, we can teach only 180 lessons on writing, on reading, on math, and so forth. Rather than fuss about all we can't get to, or dilute learning by teaching too many things in one lesson, we must hold on to what we most want our kids to know by June and work our way back from there.

TWO MINI-LESSONS THAT GREW FROM CONFERENCES

In conferences and mini-lessons, we must decide not only what to teach, but also how to teach it. Let's look at a transcript of a mini-lesson in a punctuation unit to see how one third-grade teacher, Grace Heske, did just that.

The Value of Transcribing Conferences and Mini-Lessons

One of the best ways to improve teaching is to transcribe conferences and mini-lessons. This may seem like a lot of work, but it is well worth it, because you can study exactly what you did and said, and, from there, imagine other ways of approaching the situation. One transcript can yield many insights and provide fodder for weeks of discussion and reflection.

WRITING DIALOGUE: PARAGRAPH BREAKS

1. INTRODUCE THE PURPOSE OF THE LESSON

Teacher: Is everybody ready? (*Students nod.*) Good. Yesterday we started talking about how it looks on the page when authors write dialogue, when they write the actual words that come out of a character's mouth. Then I asked you to go off and find a page in your book that taught you something about what authors do. Remember? Here is a list of some of the things you found and that you told me in our share time. (*Grace puts list on the overhead projector.*) I'll read it to you.

> *They put quotation marks before and after the words characters say.*
> *They put a comma after what the character said.*
> *Some authors only use a dash or italics when someone talks.*

This is some very smart noticing. I'd like to add another one to this list that I think is very important.

Jonathan: I know what it is. Sometimes there's no comma, like when you have a question mark or an exclamation mark.

2. READ ALOUD A PASSAGE FROM A WELL-KNOWN BOOK

Teacher: Wow, I hadn't thought of that one yet, Jonathan. Good work. What I was going to say is that the words themselves are arranged a certain way. (*Puts up a transparency on which she's typed the dialogue part of a page from* Sarah, Plain and Tall *by Patricia MacLachlan.*) I'll read these lines to you and I want you to see what happens each time a new character speaks. (*Reads the page.*)

3. Have Students Work in Pairs and Share

Teacher: Turn to your partner and talk about what you noticed. (*Grace listens in on one conversation, then returns to her place in the circle.*) Okay, let's come back together. I heard these partners say something interesting. Michael and Joey, will you share?

Joey: Sure. We said that each time someone new talks, there's a new paragraph.

Michael: Yeah, so you can keep track of who's talking if you look at the new paragraphs.

Teacher: Okay. Good noticing.

4. Encourage Students to Apply the Idea in Their Own Work

Teacher: Now I know that some of you are writing some dialogue in your stories. Today I would like you to practice writing dialogue, or revising what you wrote yesterday, by making what each character says into a new paragraph. If you are working in your notebook, try this out in an old entry so you can see how it goes. Okay? So can someone tell me back what I want you to do today?

Beth: You want us to write a story with dialogue in it.

Teacher: Not quite. I want you to revise the dialogue you wrote yesterday to make it look like the dialogue in books by putting what each character says in a new paragraph. In fact, if you have a question about how it should look, you can look in the book you are reading to see how the author did it. Okay, let's get to work.

When I talked to Grace about her lesson, she said it raised some other topics to teach in mini-lessons. For example, she thought she'd take Jonathan's comment about question and exclamation marks and make that a mini-lesson. She also felt that the second item on the children's list (i.e. "They put a comma after what the character said.") wasn't clear enough and conferring had confirmed that. She planned a more focused mini-lesson showing that a comma is used only when the dialogue is followed by a speaker tag, and that, if the tag comes first, the comma goes after it.

SMART TEACHING MOVES IN GRACE'S MINI-LESSON

Grace's mini-lesson is successful because she:

◆ ties in a previous lesson's main idea by just telling it to students; she doesn't waste any time asking them "Can you guess what's in my mind?" or "Who can remember what we did yesterday?" The way she hooks the new mini-lesson to an earlier one makes it clear why she wants to teach it. She is adding one small piece to the knowledge base she had established the previous day.

◆ actually teaches students something, that a new paragraph begins with each new speaker. It is something small and seemingly insignificant, except, of course, when children do it incorrectly. And often children do it incorrectly, because we have minimized it by lumping it together with a bunch of other rules. But, by being precise, Grace helps students find examples of the rule in books and use it immediately in their writing.

◆ shows students a page from a book they know, so they can focus on getting her point rather than thinking about the story. She also leaves space for kids to talk to each other and ask each other questions, and for her to listen in to see if they were getting it. She is not out to trick any of them, but, rather, to be sure they all understand, even if that means another student giving the answer. See Ralph Petersen's wonderful book, *Life in a Crowded Place* (Heinemann), for more discussion on creating a learning community.

◆ does not give 14 examples when one will do. In other words, Grace's mini-lesson is just that: mini. She does not go off on a tangent when Jonathan comes up with a perfectly good answer. She does not add Jonathan's idea to hers, because that would dilute his idea as well as hers. Instead, she adds it to her list of possible mini-lessons, and in fact, teaches it the next day, much to Jonathan's delight.

◆ Mini-Lesson ◆   PUNCTUATING DIALOGUE: A FOLLOW-UP MINI-LESSON

1. INTRODUCE THE PURPOSE OF THE LESSON

Teacher: I've been going around looking at your writing and I'm very pleased with the work you've been doing with dialogue. Bravo! Yesterday, you all heard Jonathan say something very smart during our mini-lesson when we were talking about how dialogue looks on the page. I asked Jonathan if he would repeat it for us today and he said he would. Jonathan?

Jonathan: Um, well, I said that sometimes there's no comma after a person speaks because what they said needs a question mark or an exclamation mark. Isn't that what I said?

2. SHOW A TEACHER-GENERATED PIECE AND THINK ALOUD

Teacher: Yes, it is. Let's look at some writing. (*Puts up a piece of her own writing on the overhead projector.*) This is that story I've been working on about a girl who plays basketball even though her mother thinks it's not ladylike. This is the part where her team-mates are really getting rough. Now look at this line. I wrote: "Cut it out," Marsha said. How do you think Marsha would say that?

Various children: (*shouting*) CUT IT OUT!!!

Teacher: Well, maybe not that loudly, but certainly more than just a plain sentence. So I probably should have an exclamation mark there, and if I put an exclamation mark in, I have to take the comma out. (*Changes the marks on the overhead.*)

Lori: Why can't you have both?

Teacher: Hmmm, that's a good question. I'm not really sure; I'll have to look up the reason in a style book. Lori, write that down for my homework. But I do know that this is the way it's supposed to look, because that's what I see authors do in the books I read.

When you use an exclamation or a question mark in dialogue, you don't need the comma. In fact, you must leave the comma out.

Jonathan: Can we add that to the chart?

3. ENCOURAGE STUDENTS TO APPLY THE IDEA IN THEIR OWN WORK

Teacher: Yes, I'll add it. But first I want you all to look at your drafts. See if there are places where your characters' dialogue needs exclamation or question marks and where you need to take out the commas.

Jordana: I think I did that already.

Teacher: Good. Can you help anyone who is confused? Then you can work on your independent writing project.

Jordana: Okay.

Teacher: So let's see if this is clear. Someone tell me what I want you to do today.

Todd: You want us to reread our drafts or the entries in our notebooks and see if there are places where dialogue doesn't need commas because it needs exclamations marks. Or question marks.

Teacher: Okay. Everyone, go write.

Grace's teaching is tight and focused. She knows what she wants to teach and how she wants to teach it. She relies on a variety of ways to get her point across, and she invites her students to be co-teachers. She has worked hard to get her teaching to this point, but she continues to imagine ways she could improve and make each lesson better. She is a model for all of us who love teaching. And her students are lovers of language, including punctuation, because of Grace's teaching.

SMART TEACHING MOVES IN GRACE'S FOLLOW-UP MINI-LESSON

Grace's mini-lesson is successful because she:

- continues on the same topic and does not bounce off to something different.

- validates the student's thinking.

- shows she is a co-learner by writing in front of her students and by telling them she needs to consult a style manual.

- uses literature to demonstrate the idea.

- keeps it short and concise, and sends children off with a clear task.

- works to scaffold students' knowledge one step at a time. She teaches one thing that is small and manageable, but that is also important and that fits in with what she taught the day before.

- bases her work plans on what she sees her students need.

Mini-lessons that follow a string provide smooth movement from one point to the next. The lessons grow organically from each other, and students seem to be right on top of the material. Conferring and mini-lessons that fit together and feed each other can make teaching tight, precise, and to the point.

Things to Remember in Punctuation Mini-Lessons

- Teach only one point per lesson.

- Model from your writing, a student's writing, or a piece of literature.

- Allow students time to process the information.

- Post the information in the room so students can refer to it.

- Give students time to try out the idea before they head off to their own drafts.

CHAPTER 6

Reading and Writing by the Book

Weaving Punctuation Study into a Literature-Based Program

B ack when I went to elementary school, I learned to read according to the factory model—from basal readers containing stories that were composed from a prescribed list of words. Vocabulary was controlled, and so was punctuation. The little writing we did was as stilted and forced as the texts we read. There were few books in the classroom, and little, if any, independent reading was encouraged. We were on our own to "compose literate lives," as Lucy Calkins says (2001). We had little help on ways to make reading and writing essential parts of our lives.

While that was an efficient way to teach the maximum number of children to be "literate" with the least effort, it did not open up worlds full of reading and writing. Instead, it trained immigrant or first-generation children to be good workers: Stay in line, don't talk, keep your eyes on your paper, respond to the bells. It was the quickest way to help the hordes take their places in American society.

However, today, our society's literacy needs are more complex. The texts children read in school, whether literature anthologies or trade books, contain all the richness of language and written conventions that writers actually use. With authentic literature in classrooms comes the excitement of reading "real" stories, but also the responsibility to teach students how those texts work. The author's purpose in basal readers was to write within the constraints of vocabulary and convention. But in authentic literature, the author's purpose is much broader. Most often it is to tell a story, not to follow rules so kids won't get mixed up.

This is not to say that the rules don't matter. Rules are important guidelines that set standards for how written conventions work. But, just as I don't need to know the laws of physics before I ride a bike, I don't need to memorize punctuation rules before I start using punctuation in writing. At some point, I will learn those physics laws, and those punctuation rules, and they will make sense to me because I have seen how they work. Students who learn to read, and then write with, punctuation will most likely understand the rules when they eventually study them.

What Authors Can Teach Us About Punctuation

When students begin to understand an author's purpose, they begin to see that writers make decisions all the time. These are some of the questions an author might ask himself or herself:

- ◆ Which part of the story will I tell?

- ◆ How will I start the story?

- ◆ How can I show what happened, rather than tell it?

Writers use conventions the way composers use time signature and rhythm—to create an effect, to establish a flow or a beat, to build tension or serenity into a scene. Notice the following sentence from Patricia MacLachlan's *The Facts and Fictions of Minna Pratt*:

"As hard as Minna tried, all she could see was her mother's room, half clean, her father in a suit, tripping over books, all of them, the lot, in danger of falling into distraction."

It is no mistake that MacLachlan has the reader tripping over that sentence with its twists and turns around commas. That is, after all, what the sentence is about, and the author wants us to feel messy and cluttered as we are reading it. That's not to say we want our students writing messy and cluttered sentences! On the contrary, we want their writing to be clear. But it does help for us to know that students will meet sentences like these in their reading, and that the punctuation use often comes back to the writer's purpose.

Katie Wood Ray teaches us in her book *Wondrous Words* (NCTE, 1999) that writers craft their work using words, rhythm, sound, and conventions. Writers no more put words haphazardly on pages than painters put paint haphazardly on canvas. Punctuation is part of the craft writers use to achieve the purpose of their writing. As students study literature, they will come to know more about conventions and use them in sophisticated ways. That's not to say that using punctuation in a strictly conventional way is wrong. On the contrary, I hope that studying literature will help children do exactly that, as they come to understand that writers always use punctuation carefully. In this chapter, I share ways to use literature to help children learn about craft and conventions.

FINDING THE BOOKS YOU NEED TO INVESTIGATE PUNCTUATION

We all have favorite children's books. I confess I have mine, and often they are books I have read to a class or to my own children when they were young. But those books—wonderful as they are—may not be the best texts for investigating punctuation. It is often necessary to look for chapter books, picture books, feature articles, editorials, sports reports, advertisements, movie and book reviews, and interviews that show punctuation as a dynamic part of composition. The text should show evidence that the writer used punctuation as a primary tool of composition. We want children to see that punctuation is not something writers add after they finish writing, something they bury under the words, but, rather, an integral part of shaping meaning. This is especially important in the initial unit, where students notice what punctuation does. I like to first show students punctuation that jumps out at them, and then move them to more conventional uses. (See Chapter Two for more on initial units.) Advanced students may want to investigate subtle, or even "invisible" punctuation, for example, places where a reader slows down or stops instinctively, even when there is no mark.

Start small. Find one book you love in which the punctuation speaks clearly to you about how to read the words. I have listed some of my favorite books on pages 137–138, but be sure to make time to discover your own. As you go through the unit, you will find more books, which could become part of an "interesting punctuation usage" bin in your library. Students can use these books when they want to use punctuation as the authors did.

CONFERRING WITH STUDENTS USING LITERATURE AS A GUIDE

When staff developer Carl Anderson used to visit my room, I was always amazed by his ability to pull out just the right literature excerpt at just the right time to help a child in a conference. Later, when I asked him how he did it, he confessed to me that he always came back to two or three pieces of literature he knew well and from which he could teach many things. He didn't need to carry around a whole library of children's books; he only needed a few very rich ones.

I recommend a similar stance when using literature to teach conventions. Identify a few pieces of literature—a page from a book, one poem, part of an article, the typed text of a picture book—and mine them for all they are worth. When conferring, it is helpful to whip out a literature excerpt that matches exactly what you want to teach, even if it's to say to a child that in formal writing, writers don't do that. While it is true that there is latitude in all kinds of writing, having literature to back you up adds weight to your teaching.

Anticipating the kinds of writing your students might be doing helps you make informed decisions about selections to carry. In the end, be sure to have a good cross-section that includes:

- Formal writing such as report writing

- Realistic fiction writing, a page from a chapter book

- Picture book writing

- Essay or informational writing

- Poetry writing

- Article writing

USING AUTHORS TO HOLD STUDENTS TO A STANDARD

Sometimes students will want to play around with punctuation and, in the process, end up making a mess of meaning. That is fine, as long as they know they are just playing around. They will tell you that their writing is like Rylant or Johnston or Ringgold or Bunting or Paulsen, and in some ways it is. What they are really doing is "gesturing" toward the work those writers do, and that is a good place to start. We know those writers have intentions for using punctuation—intentions that students often do not have.

Student uses too much punctuation to express meaning.

> Tommy H.
> April 12
>
> I went to a baseball game !!!!! With my father !!! We ate hotdogs; cotton canndy; popcorn; and frenchfriys !!! My dad drank — BEER — but I had to drink Coke ... The game was long ! ; I saw (Bernie willams); and (Tino Martinez); and I saw (two) homeruns. ! The Yankees lost... I had a GREAT time !!!!!

A FRESH APPROACH *to* TEACHING PUNCTUATION

The students may be mistaking unconventional use of punctuation for "anything goes" use, or for just plain wrong use. When students do this, I tell them my concern and ask them to explain their choices.

In looking toward authors, students often see only surface evidence, such as lots of commas, without digging under the surface to get at the meaning and motivations of the author. So I also rely on my voice to help them, by reading their writing aloud and asking, "This is how your punctuation told me to read it. Is that what you wanted?" I might ask them, "What do you mean by that?" and "Tell me how this is like Jane Yolen. In what piece of her writing did she do the same thing that you want to do in yours?" If the child has a legitimate case, I am thrilled. If not, we discuss why, often in a small-group meeting, so I am not perceived as the punctuation dictator.

Take Tommy, a fourth grader in Manhattan, for example. He had sprinkled his paper with dots, dashes, and exclamation marks. He said he was writing like Jane Yolen in *Commander Toad*. When we looked at the Yolen book, we saw that she had used some of the same things Tommy was trying, but with a lot more restraint. I explained to Tommy that his overuse of punctuation was like too much salt on a hamburger—all you can taste is the seasoning, not the meat. All we could see in Tommy's story was the use of exclamation marks, in phrases such as "Wow, this is scary!" The words did not convince us.

Tommy was resistant to changing his story. Sometimes kids are. They think the 20 question marks in a row can convey all the meaning, without having to work hard on the words. This is when I like to turn the conference over to a jury of the writer's peers. Usually the two or three others will help the writer see the problem, but occasionally I am over-ruled. That's when I know I need to do a string of mini-lessons

Questions to Ask About Punctuation Intention

- How do you want your piece to sound?

- How do you think your punctuation use accomplishes that?

- Who is the author you are following?

- Can you show me a book in which he or she used punctuation this way?

- Have you conferred with at least two other class-mates to see how they would read your writing based on the punctuation you used?

- What other ways might you punctuate this sentence? Paragraph? Whole piece?

- Is your punctuation use appropriate for your genre and/or your audience?

on formal versus informal use of punctuation, and when each is appropriate. (See page 95 for a sample lesson.) I also might take the hard line with Tommy and tell him that he must revise his punctuation because it doesn't make sense. It's my responsibility as his teacher to respect him as a learner, but also to give him coaching when he needs it.

I want students to see that punctuation, along with conventional spelling, is one of the courtesies writers extend to their readers. We punctuate so our readers can read our writing, not struggle and give up. As always, I know what to teach from what I hear students say and see them do. If something is important enough, I will bring it to the whole class in a mini-lesson; if it is a small concern, or only pertains to a few students, I will gather them for a small-group lesson.

Copies of this form are available in the writing supplies corner. Students attach it to drafts to explain their decisions.

Accountability Slip

On page _____ of this writing, I used this punctuation mark

_____ the way _____

(author's name) uses it in _____

(title of book) on page #_____ . I did this because _____

_____

_____

_____

_____ .

Understanding When It's Acceptable to Be Informal With Punctuation—and When It Isn't

1. Read Aloud a Sample Text

Collect several short texts that show varying degrees of formality. Read aloud one example to the class and demonstrate how punctuation suits the author's purposes.

2. Encourage Small-Group Inquiry

Break the class into small groups to study each of the remaining texts, looking at the degree to which the author followed conventional use. Have groups note what they observe. (This fits Cambourne's principle of immersion. See this book's introduction for more information.)

3. Return to the Meeting Area for Class Share

Elicit observations from the class and create a chart. Include not only what students observed, but why they think the author followed convention to one degree or another.

4. Encourage Independent Inquiry

Send students off to examine their own books or other texts around the room, such as magazines, nonfiction picture books, and biographies. Discuss what children are noticing about how conventions differ with genre and from writer to writer. Help them compose a statement of observations about how differences contribute to understanding:

Hatesh: "Some nonfiction books have lots of punctuation so the writer can help you get the information in small chunks."

Dana: "Some nonfiction is written in long paragraphs and the writer uses punctuation just to end sentences. It's sometimes hard to stay interested when the writer doesn't help you along and use punctuation to make you stop."

Jill: "You have to look extra carefully at punctuation in poems, because the writer is screaming at you to pay attention to every tiny thing in the poem."

While I want students to see the fullness of possibilities with punctuation, I also want them to understand that certain uses are appropriate at certain times. While, in theory, any study of punctuation can improve writing in any genre, it is safe to say that stretching the rules of punctuation on a state writing test is not a good idea. I don't want children's writing to begin looking like cartoon work, all bigger than life and going for the punch line. I want their writing to have substance and thought, all the qualities of good writing including, yes, correct punctuation. It is useful to explain that certain behaviors are appropriate at certain times, like behavior expected at the holiday dinner table at Grandma's versus at a fast-food restaurant with the soccer team. Some writing tasks require more restraint in punctuation use. So it is important for the writer to have a wide range of abilities and know when to use them.

What Style Manuals Can Teach Us About Punctuation

Style manuals keep us honest or, at least, correct. I have a few in the room for times when I need to look up a point. I also use them for times I want to show information in print so a student doesn't have to take my word for it. And there are times I want to share information with a wary administrator or parent who didn't learn punctuation the way the class is being taught.

I also want students to see that there are places to go for information we seek. And, while they may not need to look up facts in second grade, by sixth or seventh, they will. So knowing what's available is invaluable. They do not need to memorize all the rules, writing every day should make them facile. But, just as baseball umpires sometimes need to consult the rulebook, writers sometimes need to consult the style book.

Guidelines for Using Literature in the Classroom

◆ Provide literature at a reading level that's appropriate for the students.

◆ Provide literature of high quality that you read aloud to students at some point.

◆ Make multiple copies available for student perusal.

◆ Have conversations regularly about the punctuation in books, perhaps by looking at one page on an overhead.

◆ Hold students accountable when they use punctuation the way an author did in a particular book. (See accountability slip on page 94.)

◆ Display charts and work samples so that students can see the ongoing thinking about punctuation in literature, especially when outside of a unit of study.

◆ Develop a simple system that makes it easy for students to call on you or a classmate for help. (See assistance slip below.)

Assistance Slip

In my writing, I want this highlighted sentence to sound like what

_____ (author's name) did on page

_____ of _____

(title of book). I don't know if it works in my writing.

Can you help me?

Using a slip like this, which students attach to a piece of writing, makes it easy for them to request help.

Resources on Punctuation for Reference and Classroom Use

- *Punctuation Plain and Simple* by Edward C. Alward and Jean A. Alward (Career Press)

- *Essentials of English Grammar, Second Edition* by Sue L. Baugh (Passport)

- *A Dictionary of Modern English Usage* by H.W. Fowler (Oxford)

- *The New Well-Tempered Sentence* by Karen Elizabeth Gordon (Ticknor & Fields)

- *Woe Is I* by Patricia T. O'Connor (G.P. Putnam's Sons)

- *Pause and Effect: An Introduction to the History of Punctuation in the West* by M.B. Marker (University of California Press)

- *Usage and Abusage* by Eric Partridge (Norton)

- *Punctuate It Right! Second Edition* by Harry Shaw (HarperCollins)

- *Grammar Smart* by the Staff of the Princeton Review

- *Grammatically Correct* by Anne Stilman (Writers Digest Books)

- *The Elements of Style* by William Strunk, Jr. and E.B. White (MacMillan)

- *Punctuation Power: Punctuation and How to Use It* by Marvin Terban (Scholastic)

- *Write It Right!: A Desktop Digest of Punctuation, Grammar, and Style* by Jan Venolia (Ten Speed Press)

TEACHING STUDENTS TO USE STYLE MANUALS

There are occasions when students need to look up punctuation. Sometimes the way to punctuate writing is not apparent from looking at books or playing around with the punctuation marks. While most of the style manuals are written on a level far above the heads of second to fifth grade children, the information is valuable. Children should know these manuals are available to them.

Find a particularly clear and well-written manual to lean upon as a standard in the room. I prefer *The Elements of Style* by William Strunk, Jr., and E.B. White. Each of the points in this book is made clearly and often with humor. You might take one point that is relevant to your string of mini-lessons or informs children's questions, and write it on chart paper, such as Rule #3: "Enclose parenthetic expressions between commas." I would reword it in a kid-friendly way, add examples from books children know well, and invite children to add sentences from their writing as well. Later, compile the information into a class Strunk and White scrapbook. (See Appendix D.)

Chart Inspired by Strunk and White's *The Elements of Style*

What Bill and E.B. say:

If you are sticking in some extra information for the reader, put it inside two commas so he or she will know it's extra stuff. Like this:

- Mrs. Angelillo, the teacher, came to see us today.
- Do you want to go with me, after school, to the park?
- Lizards need a few things, like water and sun, to be happy.

In an ideal world, we would all have writers beside us, helping our students learn to use writers' tools. Until this happens, though, we have to do the next best thing. We have to bring in the best literature to teach children what they need to know. We have to refer to it again and again. And we have to show students that learning to use punctuation is a life-long study that continues to grow.

CHAPTER 7

Passionate About Punctuation

Conducting Advanced Studies

I never cease to be amazed by how much I learn from students when I take time to listen to them. Often I am so rushed that I pass over the smart ideas that come from them. Sometimes I misinterpret their comments, because I assume children can't be that wise, or because they explain an idea in a roundabout, original way that doesn't match my thinking. But, when I give children time to show me what they mean or say it in a way that gives me a mental picture, I see hidden things open up right before my eyes.

When I began studying the teaching of punctuation with my colleague Isoke Nia, I assumed that students would learn to use punctuation in their reading and writing. But, I confess, I didn't consider that they might become so fascinated by punctuation that they might want to continue studying it. I didn't realize that their curiosity could bring them to deeper studies of punctuation.

In Rachel Bard's classroom, one of her fourth graders, Juan, casually commented on something that led to new investigations. Juan had read Ralph Fletcher's novels *Flying Solo* and *Fig Pudding*, as well as the children's writing books, *A Writer's Notebook* and *Live Writing*. In a conference, Juan told Rachel he had noticed that Fletcher uses punctuation differently depending on the genre. His poetry is punctuated differently from his novels, which are, in turn, punctuated differently from his books about writing.

When Rachel asked Juan if he would be interested in studying more deeply the variations in Fletcher's punctuation use, he said no. He was more interested in picking a genre and studying how different authors used punctuation within it. Specifically, he wanted to explore how writers use punctuation to make informational texts, such as *A Writer's Notebook*, interesting. Thus, a new kind of study was born: the "punctuation within a genre" study.

Punctuation Within a Genre
A Mid-Year Study

In response to Juan's discovery, and the way it piqued the students' interest, Rachel and I planned our second unit of study at the middle of the year. We decided not to do an author study, but rather a study on punctuation use within genre writing. We asked the students to look over books in the classroom library to decide what genres they might want to study. We made it clear that genres they had already studied might work best, but that they were welcome to look at unfamiliar ones, too. The students came up with the following list:

- Poetry
- Memoir
- Nonfiction informational books

- Funny chapter books
- Sports writing
- Editorials

Students then signed up for the genres they wanted to study. They formed groups based on their selections and went off to investigate the ways writers used punctuation within those genres. (We would have permitted individual study of a genre, but no one expressed interest in working alone.)

Some of the boys were very interested in sports writing. They read the sports pages in *The New York Post* and *The Daily News*, intent on following the New York Knicks every step of the way to the playoffs. They noticed that sports writing tends to capture the excitement of the game, often because of the writers' use of short sentences that build suspense and punctuation that mimics the fast pace of the players. They compared the writing of sports journalists Mike Lupica and Dick Shapp. They listened to sports reporters summarizing games on radio and television and imagined how their words might be punctuated. The boys concluded that this genre is most successful when writers use words and punctuation that keep the writing lively and as fast-paced as the games they describe. They used Lupica and Shapp as mentors for their own writing, and created a newspaper of their own, *Sports Unillustrated*.

Another group was interested in informational writing. Three students in this group were fascinated by snakes and had read several books about them. The other two were interested in large mammals and in severe weather. The group went to

---

Punctuation in Informational Books

- A lot of the punctuation is conventional. It's a good genre to study for regular punctuation, like you need when you write reports or essays.

- When writers are telling you stories (anecdotes) to show something, they use short sentences and lots of punctuation to build suspense or drama.

- Writers use punctuation to tell you what information to pay attention to, like a colon tells you that an explanation or definition comes next.

- Writers use dialogue and quotation marks to break up the print in long passages of information. This makes it easier to read.

the class library and gathered short chapter books and picture books they had read, as well as some new books. They looked over the books to find text features that helped them read effectively, such as captions, bold print, italics, and charts. Then they looked at the punctuation and talked about how it helped them understand the information. They made the chart on page 102, based on their findings.

The other groups in Rachel's class made similar charts based on what they had discovered. The study culminated with each group displaying its chart and explaining its findings to the class. The students concluded that effective writers of any genre use the tool of punctuation with care and purpose.

Year-End Studies

READING ACROSS GENRES WITH A PUNCTUATION FOCUS

Students often read wondering only, "What is this about?" Rachel and I want our students to wonder also, "How does the punctuation inform my ideas about what this is about?" So, when we return to punctuation at the end of the year, we begin a study with that goal in mind.

In the mid-year advanced study, students notice how punctuation is used in the individual genres they study, as well as how and when it is not used. Now, over the course of two weeks, we want them to look across examples of each genre to form theories about the ways writers use punctuation to help readers hear the "sound" of those genres and gain meaning from them.

Since Rachel reads aloud to her children all year, they know that essays sound different from articles, which sound different from poems, which sound different from editorials. We hope they see what is acceptable or customary within certain genres and what is not. It is not enough for students to say, "We saw more semicolons in this essay than in that poem;" they need to come up with theories about why that is so. ("It is accepted practice?" "It is traditionally done that way?" "The writer wanted to achieve more complex meaning?" "The writer was more skilled?" and so forth.)

Gathering Interesting Multi-Genre Writing Samples

Always be on the lookout for interesting writing, ready to cut out articles, editorials, ads, profiles, and any other compelling pieces that come your way. When I visit other cities or countries, I often find unusual samples of writing; even airline magazines are filled with short, lively pieces of high interest. Just being in a new place and getting a different perspective causes me to read with a different perspective.

We know punctuation use alone doesn't create these differences among genres. But we want students to investigate it as one variable. Indeed, there are many angles from which to study forms of writing, and punctuation is only one. We could focus on many others, such as word choice, sentence length, voice, use of grammar, theme, tone, mood, and elements of story. Although we single out punctuation, it would be odd, if not a downright literary crime, to look always and only at the punctuation in a piece of writing. We, as teachers, must develop eyes that see many things in student writing; we must see beyond the "mechanics," or at least, we should see written conventions in insightful ways. And we must teach our students to do the same.

Rachel chooses powerful writing samples in 10 genres, which students had studied before for other purposes. She photocopies them and places them into individual files. Over the next three days, in small groups, students choose four of the 10 genres to study, using the samples in the files. The students lay the samples across their desks to notice differences and similarities in punctuation use. Students write down their observations, as well as thoughts on how the punctuation use they notice informs their own writing. (See sample on page 105 and Appendix E.)

After students study the file samples, the are invited to go into the class or school library to find examples that either confirm or dispute their findings. They write these examples on index cards and attach them to genre-specific charts. All students are expected to contribute one example to each of the four genres they are studying, with a short explanation of what they have found, as well as a citation.

On day eight of the study, Rachel and I ask group members to intermingle for conversations about punctuation across genres. The conversations focus on how acceptable punctuation use in each genre often differs, and that writers really know how to use punctuation as a tool.

Transcript of a Conversation Between Jorge, Samantha, and William:

Jorge: Well, my first study group was the sports writing group, and we had looked at the punctuation in sports articles. So I wanted to see what other writing had the same kind of punctuation—you know, exciting punctuation.

William: My first group studied editorials from the newspaper and magazines. We had thought they would be pretty, you know, calm and usual about punctuation, but we found out that they can be pretty lively. Especially if there is something they are really angry about. Though sometimes it makes a difference which paper you read. Like the Post doesn't worry about being perfect the way the editors do in Ms. Bard's New York Times.

Samantha: When were you reading The New York Times?

William: I wasn't reading it. Ms. Bard showed it to me and I saw what they did on the editorial page.

Jorge: Did you look at the sports pages?

William: No.

Jorge: Let's do that! Maybe it makes a difference by newspaper as well as genre.

Samantha: Wait—not now. I got to talk about my stuff first. We did poetry in our first study, and the punctuation was all over the place. At first we thought that poets just do, you know, whatever they want and they don't worry about who's going to like it or not. But then we picked a few poems and read them really

Fourth graders report on punctuation study in four genres

Name: Katie

Punctuation Study in Four Genres

Four Genres	Memoir	Poetry	Editorial	Feature Article
What I noticed About punctuation	it tries to slow you down at good parts so you enjoy it.	a little bit of punctuation, because white space helps me read poem	punctuation helps the writers voice come through so it sounds like he's talking to you.	fonts change to tell whats important
Example from Literature	Rylant My Grandmothers Hair	Naomi Nye poems & Carl Sandburg Poems	School Bullies	"Soap"
What this means for my writing	to figure out whats the really good part of my memoir and then slow it down with dashes and ellipsis.	be careful with the punctuation and read poems out loud for how they sound	use questions to make reader feel like I'm talking	change font when I want the reader to pay attention
Example from my Writing	My uncle held my hand he was frail and cold. I know that it would soon end.	I go to my house: it's dark and it's cold.	Don't you think guns are dangerous? Don't you think enough kids have died?	when you skate, you have to practice keeping your ankles straight.

carefully, and we decided that the poets were using punctuation very carefully. We think the punctuation counts more in poetry than in other writing, because there isn't too much writing in a poem, so that everything the poet does probably counts. But if you're writing a whole book, you can waste a few commas. That's what I think after I looked at samples from chapter books and from a biography.

Jorge: That's crazy. Why would you waste commas? Don't you know better by now? (*laughs*)

Samantha: I didn't say I would waste them . . .

William: Okay, let's get back to this. I have an editorial here from *Newsday*, and it's written like the editor was talking to you. Actually, it's like he was grabbing you by the collar and saying that if you don't agree, you can leave town. So the punctuation is in there to make it sound like he's talking to you, or yelling at you. You can hear him stopping for a breath here and there when he uses commas and dashes. And here there is one sentence that goes on too long because he wants us to feel suspense.

Jorge: Maybe he forgot to put the periods in.

Building in Self-Evaluation

At the end of the study in Rachel's class, we ask the children to reflect on their learning. This is a way for us to check on our teaching as well, so we can think about ways to teach better. Their reflections are interesting testimonies to how much they have learned. They are no longer worried about getting the punctuation "wrong" or writing painfully simple sentences to avoid making mistakes. They have come to realize that punctuation is a writer's tool, like a carpenter's hammer. They are thinking about punctuation in different genres. And they are using punctuation like writers. (See student evaluation on page 107.)

A FRESH APPROACH *to* TEACHING PUNCTUATION

Name: *Mark*
Title of writing: *My Grandfathers Illness*
Date: *March 20*

Self-evaluation in punctuation

One place where I used punctuation as I wrote to help me shape meaning is: *Where I wrote the scene about my grandfather drooling and making a mess*

One place where I used a mentor text to help me punctuate is: *I wanted to slow down the part in the hospital so I used the dashes and commas like the first page of Night in the country.*
The mentor text I studied and used is:
Night in the country

One way I use punctuation well is:
I always use quotation marks for talking.

One way I tried to use punctuation that is new for me is:
I tried to use dashes.

One punctuation thing I want to work on is:
Getting commas in the right places.

Mark evaluates his use of punctuation. (See Appendix F for a reproducible template.)

Samantha: Stop it, Jorge. They couldn't print it if it wasn't right.

Jorge: I don't know about that.

Samantha: So let's see if we can say something about which genre is strict and which is not strict with punctuation.

William: I don't know if we can do that. It probably depends on the writer.

Samantha: Let's try.

Jorge: Well, we could say some general stuff. So we could know when to be really strict, you know.

William: Yeah, let's do it.

In the end, one group got together and constructed a "continuum" for punctuation use across genres. Members presented it to the class and students spent time looking for samples that would confirm or refute their findings.

Least conventional							Most conventional
free writing	poetry	sports	editorial	feature article	news article	school report	state test

This study is very powerful. For some struggling students, it may be the first time the idea of writing with a purpose really "clicks." They hear and see the differences among the genres, partly because the punctuation use creates different rhythms, and partly because setting samples of four genres next to each other forces them to see that poems and feature articles and editorials and sports articles look, as well as sound, different. They have the chance to listen to the music of the writing and think about how punctuation helps achieve it.

FOCUSING ON PUNCTUATION WITHIN AN EXTENDED, SINGLE-GENRE STUDY

In the study we did in Rachel's class, instruction centers exclusively on punctuation use across genres. Another way to structure an advanced punctuation study is to make it a short part of a larger, whole-class, extended study of a single genre. In a poetry study, for example, the class can look at how poets use punctuation in their work, along with other tools. In such a study, the genre itself, not the punctuation, is the focus. Mini-lessons can center around all aspects of writing poetry, including punctuation. Both approaches are effective. Base your choice on where the class's interest lies and/or where you see the area of greatest need.

To do the punctuation study within a genre study, ask students to pay close attention to the punctuation in the class touchstone texts and/or in their mentor texts. (See page 63 for definitions of these texts.) Plan several mini-lessons that demonstrate how you, as a poet for example, might use punctuation to shape meaning and the reader's interpretation of your poem. Also, show several well-known poems on overhead transparencies or charts to illustrate how punctuation shapes reading. Ask students to talk about what they see and how it directs their reading of the poem. Mark their observations on the text and use them to construct a general chart of ways poets use punctuation. (See the sample chart below that a second-grade class created during their springtime poetry study.)

In a genre study, students read widely within the genre and are expected to produce writing in that genre. Therefore, ask students to make observations about ways their mentor writers of the genre use punctuation. Ask them, also, why they made some of the punctuation choices they did in their own writing. Punctuation awareness adds a rich dimension to a genre study, although, clearly, it should not be the sole focus.

Using Punctuation in Poetry

- ◆ *Use it to make your reader take a breath*

- ◆ *Use it to make your reader slow down*

- ◆ *Think about each mark before you use it*

- ◆ *Choose punctuation carefully, like words*

- ◆ *Ask a friend to read your poem the way you punctuated it*

USING PUNCTUATION AS A REVISION STRATEGY

Revisiting and revising writing from earlier in the year is another way to approach advanced punctuation study. Leslie Feldman and I do this in her fourth-grade class toward the end of the school year. The purpose of the study is to look at what punctuation can do to help students to "resee" and, therefore, revise their writing.

First, we make sure students understand what we mean when we tell them to revise their work using punctuation. We often believe that editing is the only point at which writers "check over" their punctuation. But writers think about punctuation, as well as the words, sentences, and paragraphs, as they write. Therefore, students need to see that punctuation is a primary act of composition, and that

> P.S.21   1st Draft
> 5-324   10/30
>
> ### My mom's childhood
>
> When my mom was young, she had a happy
> life. Even if she (all the girls) did not go to
> school, she (they) had a hard life. That
> time only boys could go to School
>   My mom also had a boring life,
> but   my   mom   said," I   had a wonder
> ful life, in summer me and my fri
> ends would go to the lake and
> swim, catch frogs and bugs. In winter
> we   would   go out! to play in the
> snow.
>   It's pretty hard to believe, but
> it's true. Sometimes I make believe
> I am my mom when she was young
> It is fun! In summer my mom
> would put out the mini air pool
> at   the   balquinie, and I would
> put little toys in the water and
> preatend thoose are little bugs, and
> I try to catch them.
>   But it is boring to only play
> by myself. So I bring friends

they should use punctuation as they compose to help them shape meaning. In addition, writers reread continually as they write, working to get their writing closer to exactly what they want to say. Often the act of writing itself helps them clarify their thinking. So, in pieces the students have already completed, we ask them to revise—that is, to rethink and rewrite—putting the punctuation to work, rather than just changing some of the marks and considering their work finished. We want evidence that punctuation is becoming part of the way students think as writers.

To get students started, Leslie conducts the following mini-lesson.

Revisiting and Revising Writing, Grade 4

1. Introduce the Purpose of the Lesson

Leslie puts a piece of her own writing on the overhead projector, a memoir she wrote in October. Now, in May, she is looking at it with some distance. (This, in itself, is a good habit to teach students. Many writers put manuscripts away for a few weeks or months before revising.) Leslie tells the class that there are lots of ways she can revise her memoir. She lists several of them, including:

◆   Slowing down the good parts

◆   Starting at a different place in the story

◆   Adding some dialogue.

Then she explains that, because she has learned so much about punctuation during the school year, she particularly wants to look at the writing from that angle.

2. Model the Revision Strategy

Leslie thinks aloud in front of the class. She notices that she has used very few punctuation marks to shape her writing, and that the punctuation she has used doesn't seem to help drive the story along. So she revises the writing on the overhead, talking about the effect she wants and how punctuation can help her achieve it. Notice how attention to what punctuation can do changes Leslie's writing.

Leslie explains that thinking about how punctuation helps her tell the story inspires her to change not only the punctuation, but the words, too.

Leslie's Memoir, Original and Revised Versions

Original Version:

Grandpa sat at our table every night after dinner and told stories. He told sad stories and funny stories and true stories and ghost stories. All around him, people sat, laughing or just listening, their eyes and ears all his. Except for me. I was alone in the crowd. I watched their faces. I saw them smile. I heard them laugh. But I couldn't hear the stories.

My Grandpa only spoke Yiddish. And I only spoke English.

Revised Version:

"Brrinngg!" The doorbell rang and the neighbors poured in. Words flew all around me—fast, harsh, loud sounds–but I watched their faces to understand them. The words were foreign to me; they were strange and awkward to my ears. I watched their smiles, their eyes, their arms and hands as they talked. I knew they were all there for one reason: they were there to hear Grandpa's nightly stories.

Soon the crowd settled at our large oak table. Mama cleared the dirty dinner dishes, while Grandpa took his place at the head. Papa shouted at him—"Tell the one about . . ." or "No! Tell the one about . . ."—but Grandpa had his own ideas. He knew what mood he was in . . . funny, scary, sad, dangerous. He could tell stories from the Old Country, or from the long trip over, or from the hard life here. He could tell anything. Anything at all. It didn't matter, because they loved every minute.

And it didn't matter to me either: whatever story he chose to tell would remain a mystery to me.

I couldn't understand a word of it. I couldn't understand Grandpa's Yiddish tales. I was deaf to his language.

3. ENCOURAGE STUDENTS TO APPLY THE IDEA IN THEIR OWN WORK

After the lesson, students go to their writing folders, in which they store all their writing from the school year, and choose a piece to revise for punctuation. They are surprised at how much they've learned in general about writing. Some even comment that they were "very new writers in October." Most find ways to revise using punctuation to shape meaning. (See sample below.)

Ariel
4-403
~~October 4, 1999~~ May 14

My brother is a pest, and he gets me mad.
Sometimes he yells in my ears and pushes me down.
The worst thing he does is he tells lies about me
to my mother. Then she says, go to your room and
cool down, but I'm not the one who was bad. I'm only
mad at him. When I tell my mother she says, he's just
a little boy, but I know he understands. He gets me
in trouble for nothing

    Sometimes I take him to the park and I play
with him. But If he doesn't want to go home he cries
and tells my mother I punched him. So I don't want
to take him to the park anymore, but I want to love
him.

    Why do little kids do things like this? Why
can't he be nice? We could have lots of fun. Then
I would give him my dolls and play Legos with him
if he wanted. But now I am just frustrated with him.

What I did was put in the punc. I was
     leaving out.

What else I want to do is put more dialog,
     like what I said, and description in
     the park.

Now I can write more than I could then.

Ariel revises work after several months of learning about punctuation and writing.

REVISING AND REVISING WRITING, GRADE 2

The following is a transcript of a mini-lesson that second-grade teacher Karen Kessler included in a unit of study on revision. The students are gathered around her in the meeting area.

1. INTRODUCE THE PURPOSE OF THE LESSON

Teacher: Boys and girls, yesterday we talked about the author examples you have been gathering to add to our punctuation charts. We said that the charts would be so much richer if we included examples from many different writers. So, after school, when I looked at the charts, and I was happy to see examples from so many different writers. Let's see. We have Seymour Simon, Patricia Reilly Giff, Valerie Worth, Patricia MacLachlan. Last night I was thinking that you have already learned so much from these authors about the ways punctuation is used in different genres that it's probably time for you to try some of it out in your own writing. Now I know that not all of you have had a chance to add your author examples to all the charts, so that is something you can work on today. But the thing I want to talk about today is how writers go back to revise their work. Seeing what other writers have done—like the author examples you wrote on our punctuation charts—can help us figure out some things we can do in our own writing.

2. ENCOURAGE DIALOGUE AROUND A PIECE OF STUDENT WRITING

Teacher: Here is the poem Anna wrote when we studied poetry. She said that we can look at it. (*Karen puts Anna's writing up, which she printed on chart paper ahead of time.*) Anna said she would be happy to revise her work for you. Come, Anna. (*Anna comes up and*

Karen hands her a green marker.)

Anna: Well, I was thinking that I like the way Valerie Worth uses very little punctuation. So, in my poem, I think I want to take out the commas I put at the end of every line. I think I only did that because that's what I thought poets do. So I'm going to cross them out.

Alex: But if you take out all the punctuation, we won't have any idea how to read it.

Anna: I'm going to leave the period in at the end.

Alex: I think you could read it and if there is another place where you want us to go slow, you could put a comma there.

Brigid: Or you could put a dash. A dash would make us slow down.

Anna: I like dashes.

Brigid: Yeah, but don't use too many of them. Only use one.

Anna: Okay. Then I would be like Valerie Worth.

Alex: You still need some commas.

Anna: Where?

Alex: After the word "foot."

Anna: Well, I'll try it there and if I like it, I'll let it stay. (*adds in the punctuation*)

Teacher: Thank you, Anna.

Before

Anna F.

My cat hcls feet
That look like black pebbles
But they are soft
And smooth
And cold.
When I hold
    one foot
He pushes me with the other feet
Then he runs away to play.

After

Anna F.

My cat hcls feet
That look like black pebbles,
But they are soft...
And smooth...
And cold.
When I hold
    one foot,
He pushes me with the other feet.
Then he runs away to play.

Anna's poem before and after she worked on punctuation

Teeth

My teeth are litte and they Fall
Out of My mouth .
teeth dont come out of
big peopels mouth .
Ouly when they get old their
teeth come out again and old
people die .

3. HAVE STUDENTS SHARE IN PAIRS

Teacher: So, writers, what I would like you to do today is to go back to your writing folder and take out a piece you have already finished. It could be something you wrote in one of our genre studies, or an independent piece you did. Try to revise your work by doing some of the things with punctuation that the writers we've studied have done. Please write down the reason you made the change on a stick-on note and leave the piece and the note in my box. Do you understand? Okay, could you all turn to your partners and talk about how you imagine this might go today in your writing. (*Karen listens in on the conversations.*)

4. ENCOURAGE STUDENTS TO APPLY THE IDEA IN THEIR OWN WORK

Teacher: Let's come back together everyone. I heard some interesting plans when I listened in. I heard someone say she wants to revise her poem to look like Pat Mora's poem "Mountain Silhouette." I heard someone else say he wants to change the punctuation in his editorial on school uniforms to make the rhythm faster. These are some good plans. Okay, go work quietly and I'll be around for conferences.

A FRESH APPROACH *to* TEACHING PUNCTUATION

Karen's mini-lesson demonstrates that she is carefully studying what students are doing every day, and adjusting her teaching accordingly. Notice how she allows them to rehearse by planning with a partner before sending them off to try the strategy on their own. She also makes it clear that finishing assigned work quickly does not mean they're done. There is always other work they can go back to, other drafts to revise. Karen is building independence in her second graders, as well as shaping and scaffolding their learning.

Carrying Out Independent Studies in Punctuation

I often visit classes where students are doing a good job at punctuation, using it correctly, or at least thoughtfully, in much of their writing. And, every once in a while, there are a few students who are truly fascinated by punctuation and interested in learning more. We nurture the science interests of a future physicist and biologists in our rooms, and also those of language lovers—future writers, editors, and English teachers. For these students, we have designed studies to continue expanding their expertise. Most often, students take on these studies individually or in small independent study groups.

It is important for students to understand that participation in an independent study is voluntary, because the work will be hard and sophisticated. It requires commitment on the part of the students and a clear timeframe assures that the study will not fall apart prematurely. A short letter to parents explaining the study and asking for their assistance can make the study manageable. As in any work we do, it is always wise to keep parents informed, so they are able to support it at home.

GUIDELINES FOR INDEPENDENT STUDIES

There are some general guidelines you should follow for any small-group independent work so you can hold students accountable for their use of time and keep in touch with what they are doing.

Possible Independent Study Topics

- How one author, such as Gary Paulsen, uses punctuation for style

- How one author's use of punctuation compares to another author's, for example Patricia MacLachlan's to Gary Paulsen's

- How punctuation changes over time, either in general sense or in the history of a particular author

- Deeper study of a particular mark

- How to read when there is little or no punctuation to guide you

- How we learn how to read "invisible" punctuation, that is, places in text where we instinctively pause even if there is no punctuation

- How two or more style manuals compare

- How punctuation is changing today because of computers and e-mail

- Punctuation in languages other than English

- How a student's own punctuation use changes over time

- Genres not already studied by the class

- Punctuation in political cartoons and comic strips

After you explain the purposes and possibilities of independent studies, interested students should write a very short proposal for their inquiry to get your approval. The proposal should include the timeframe for the study and the "product" the group will produce at the end. Once the proposal is approved, the student posts an advertisement on a bulletin board for others to join the study. Interested students can sign up and should be told of the commitment in terms of time and work. Give students time to meet, plan out the project, and decide how they will work together. For example, will the study require library visits? Meetings after school? Teacher guidance?

Give students a daily portion of writing workshop time to work on their inquiry. At the end of their study, they might produce a short summary of their findings, including literature references, in the form of a chart or a large index card.

Independent Study in Punctuation

Name(s) of people in group:

Kevin   Mark
Allison Adrienne

What we are studying:

Punctuation in emails

How we plan to find out what we want to know:

- look at lots of emails
- interview people who write emails

Some books we might use:

There are no emails in books, but we could look at Bill & EB to check the rules that emailers are breaking.

What we are thinking and why:

email looks different from school w[o] because people are writing fast and do[n] pay careful attention.

Some possible conclusions (fill this out as you near end of study):

Maybe punctuation will disappear someday because people will get used to not having it
Or it will look different.

Members of an independent study group plan their work. (See Appendix G for a reproducible template.)

Laminate the work and add it to a class inquiry-results archive. Students could also visit other groups within or outside of the class to talk about their findings. In almost every case, children experience exhilaration at having designed and completed an inquiry into something they care about deeply.

Sample Independent Study: Punctuation Use in E-mail

Five children in Alcira Jaar's fourth-grade class wanted to study how punctuation is changing today because of computers and electronic mail. They agreed to print out e-mails they received for one week and bring them in for investigation. They made copies and laid the e-mails out on the rug. As it turned out, not one of the e-mail letters they had received contained capital letters or apostrophes. Alcira and I acted shocked, but, in reality, we knew that many people disregard such conventions in their e-mails. The children then printed out Instant Messages they received, and concluded that the use of punctuation in them was even less conventional than in traditional e-mails. They decided that the informality and speed of electronic mail made it acceptable for people to bend written conventions a little. Omar even suggested that perhaps in a dozen or so years, capital letters and apostrophes will disappear from all writing. Alcira and I doubt it, but we'll see.

After a study of how punctuation compares in different languages, three children in Rachel Bard's classroom summed up how they felt. "We figured this out ourselves," they said. "We knew there were some differences in the way punctuation is used in Spanish and how it is used in English, and we wanted to teach that to other kids. Now we have a list of the ways they are different. You can come to us if you need some answers."

How empowering it is for children to find something that fascinates them, design a way to explore it, and discover answers to their own questions. Many educators believe that learning this way helps students see relevance in their work and creates knowledge that will last throughout their school careers and beyond.

CHAPTER 8

Losing the Red Pen

Evaluating Written Conventions

When I was in third grade, I had a teacher who believed there was some moral goodness attached to the correct use of written conventions. Any writing that was not "perfect" was, by definition, "bad writing," and students who had trouble with conventions were, well, "of limited capacity." I recall the humiliation of getting back my papers splashed with the blood-red marks of her correction pen, with remarks like, "You need to work on punctuation" scrawled across my words. Fortunately, few teachers still believe that tormenting young writers improves writing, but many do wonder how to point out errors to children in ways that nudge them toward more conventional use.

Mina Shaughnessy (1977) tells us that errors are opportunities for us to learn more about a child, to investigate what the child is thinking and how the child's learning is moving forward. Errors are not, in and of themselves, bad. They are ways for us to find out what is happening inside the child's mind, the complicated cognitive work that goes into learning something. Similarly, Yetta Goodman (1987) and Sandra Wilde (2000) studied children's reading "miscues," or errors, and show us how we can learn much about learners from them. William Strong (1999) tells us it is dishonest to invite risk taking and then penalize students for taking risks.

Given what these thinkers have taught us, the way we look at student's punctuation use must change. It is no longer sufficient for us to "correct" children's punctuation errors without looking at them closely to analyze the reasons behind those mistakes. And, while few of us still bloody the pages with red pens, we can do the same damage with blue or green pens and with our lack of thoughtfulness about what student errors mean.

However, if we set aside blocks of time for deep study of punctuation, rather than tacking it on and expecting students to get it right, we will be more thoughtful in the ways we evaluate students' work. In fact, I suspect those students will make fewer errors in the long run. That said, it would be naïve to think that children will not make errors. When we study those errors, we must ask thoughtful questions:

- What do the errors say about what the student knows about punctuation?

- What is the student trying to do here?

- How can I help the student accomplish his or her goal?

- What are the next steps for the student?

It's important to accept that fact that children will make punctuation errors as they attempt to write more complicated sentences, just as they will make errors in grammar. We must think of punctuation as an ongoing skill to be continually refined and mastered as children grow as writers.

Furthermore, we must begin to treat written conventions as something important. For so long we have treated them in a perfunctory way, giving children the subtle message these rules are insignificant and not worth much of our attention. Then we grade their papers and find so much to "correct." No wonder students are confused: Are written conventions important or aren't they? If they are important, why don't we spend more time on them? If they're not, why do teachers typically get so upset when students make mistakes? I can understand their confusion, since I am confronted with mixed messages all the time in the teachers' rooms I visit. In this chapter, I share ways to evaluate students' work with an eye toward clearing up that confusion and helping students become better writers.

Using Rubrics for Evaluation

Rubrics are a good way to look at conventions; in fact, they are a good way to evaluate all aspects of writing. The most effective rubrics match the work that's being done in the room. They should be constructed by the teacher and students together, and clearly name the points upon which work will be evaluated. They should also be cumulative to capture all the teaching and learning that happens between, say, October and March. Here is a sample punctuation rubric designed by a fourth-grade class and how it evolved as the year passed:

RUBRIC
Written Conventions: October

Convention	Writer	Student Editor	Teacher
I write in full sentences.			
I use ending punctuation.			
I studied a mentor author.			
One thing I think I need to work on is: _____.			

RUBRIC

Written Conventions: December

Convention	Writer	Student Editor	Teacher
I write in full sentences.			
I use ending punctuation.			
I write in paragraphs.			
I use commas in dialogue.			
I use commas in lists.			
I studied a mentor author.			

One thing I need to work on is: _____.

I learned this from my mentor author: _____.

Tips for Developing Rubrics

◆ Align rubrics with what you have taught in your mini-lessons.

◆ Ask students to compose rubrics with you.

◆ Be sure the criteria are clear.

◆ Leave space for more than one evaluator, such as another student or a staff member.

◆ Be sure rubrics represent learning that the student is attempting to do, as well as "mastery."

◆ Keep rubrics simple and short.

◆ Revise rubrics as students become more sophisticated.

RUBRIC

Written Conventions: April

Convention	Writer	Student Editor	Teacher
I use the correct ending punctuation.			
I use commas to control my sentences.			
I write in paragraphs.			
I use other marks correctly:			
-apostrophes			
-dashes			
-semicolons			

I am studying a mentor author.

Something I tried in this
writing that was new is:_____ .

Something I want to work
on for next time is: _____ .

A writer I will study next is:_____ .

Other Ways to Evaluate Punctuation

Rubrics give us one piece of the puzzle as we attempt to understand what students are learning. But they do not give us enough information to understand deeply what children are doing. Here are some other ways to gather information for evaluation:

- ◆ Accumulate each student's writing over the year and keep it in a folder for periodic evaluation.

- ◆ Schedule regular conferences that focus on written conventions.

- ◆ Call together small groups for punctuation conversations, while you listen in. Ask students to look over their work in advance and take notes to prepare.

- ◆ Collect dictation and study it.

- ◆ Examine draft writing versus published writing.

- ◆ Ask students to write brief self-evaluations of punctuation use.

- ◆ Ask students to write plans for improving their punctuation work and use those plans to evaluate progress.

ACCUMULATE EACH STUDENT'S WRITING OVER THE YEAR AND KEEP IT IN A FOLDER FOR PERIODIC EVALUATION

About every six to eight weeks, take out a student's folder and spread the work on a table. Choose one area of punctuation the student has been working on; you should be able to get this information from your conferring notes. Then look at it

Sample Notes: Leona, Grade 2

9/25:   no punctuation, including capital letters

10/30:   capital letters at beginning of sentences and proper names, no periods

11/18:   periods at end of every line, evidence of self-correction; I told her to look in her independent reading book, Rylant's Poppleton, to study periods.

11/28:   periods at end of most sentences, some capitals. Using peer editor. Able to show 2 pages in Poppleton where she studied periods.

12/20:   capitals, periods/sentence ends all good, but no commas. Told her to study Poppleton for commas.

1/30:   commas in a series, attempting apostrophes

2/20:   apostrophes good!

These brief notes provide a clear view into Leona's growing punctuation knowledge, as well as her use of the resources in the room to help her. The teacher also noted that Leona was not using literature as a guide, but that she was able to talk about some of the decisions she made. Leona is clearly improving, and her teacher is keeping a close eye on her progress.

across the papers. Again, keep notes on what you notice to help you plan instruction and to help at parent conferences.

Between parent conferences, send home photocopies of published pieces, because parents are gratified to see their child's work and some even fear there isn't enough work going on if they don't see it coming home. Keep all originals in an archival file in the room.

SCHEDULE REGULAR CONFERENCES THAT FOCUS ON WRITTEN CONVENTIONS

In general, the conferring I do with students grows from the needs I see. As I teach the writer, and not the writing (Anderson, 2000), I build ideas about what

 **J**anet listens in on a small group's conversation on punctuation.

Fitting Punctuation Conferences into Your Schedule

- Set aside a week for punctuation conferences with all students.

- Conduct follow-up punctuation conferences sporadically, but keep a record to be sure to reach each student.

- Ask students to come to at least one conference a month prepared to say something about their punctuation thinking.

writers need. Some of those ideas should be about the ways a student uses conventions.

In my classroom, I recall the difficulty of staying on top of all my writers' needs. I developed a system for keeping track of conferences, which helped me determine which children I had seen, what I had taught them, how I would hold them accountable for the work I had asked them to do, and how quickly I needed to follow up. I discovered quickly, though, that my system didn't help me determine the kinds of conferences I was having with children. It was possible, for example, for me to neglect to confer with Jose on punctuation, because whenever I met with him, we worked on keeping his writing focused. I solved the problem by tracking who I had seen and what kind of conference we had, on a sheet of graph paper at the front of my conferring notebook.

While it is a smart idea to have a theory about a student writer and to stay with it for a long while—for example, Jose needs to work on keeping his writing focused—it is also

Planning for Group Conversations

◆ Ask students to bring a piece of their own writing and discuss the punctuation decisions they made.

◆ Invite students to talk about a short shared text or touchstone text with respect to what they know about its punctuation.

◆ Urge students to bring up their questions, confusions, and even despairs about punctuation.

◆ Encourage students to share ways they solved punctuation problems they had.

◆ If students ask, clarify something you already taught or teach something they want to know.

◆ Be proud if your students have enough trust in you to question your decisions. For example, courageous children might talk about the way you graded a rubric.

important to work one-on-one with students on punctuation. To accomplish this, you might set apart a week of conferences and focus mostly on conventions for that week. Conferences, in addition to evaluating work across time, can give you lots of information about a child's thinking.

CALL TOGETHER SMALL GROUPS FOR PUNCTUATION CONVERSATIONS, WHILE YOU LISTEN IN

Look at your class list and choose a group of three or four students at varied levels. Tell the students that they will be having a 10-minute conversation in two or three days, and that they should give some thought to how they are learning punctuation. Also, tell them that you will be evaluating your own teaching, as well as their learning, by being a silent participant. Obtain their written permission to tape the conversation in case you want to study it later. I find that taping works well, because it is hard to pay attention and take careful notes at the same time.

Then listen to the students. Hear what they are saying. Be sure that the quiet voices have a place in a conversation. Take the pulse of the room. If you listen with an open mind, children will tell you more things about your teaching and their learning than you might have imagined.

COLLECT DICTATION AND STUDY IT

Collecting dictation every now and then gives you a good idea of how students are progressing and if any are having a particular difficulty. Note the kinds of errors they are making. Try to discern patterns in those errors that might reveal what the student is thinking. For example, knowing that Maria misses commas isn't very useful, but knowing that she is not hearing pauses in a list, which a dictation would reveal, tells us more specifically what we might need to teach Maria. Date dictations and keep them in the archival file in case you need to refer to them later. (For more on collecting dictation, see page 71.)

EXAMINE DRAFT WRITING VERSUS PUBLISHED WRITING

Because I want children to be using punctuation as a tool, I want them going back to drafts to think about punctuation and to change it as needed. You may want to ask students to make changes in a different-colored pencil, so that you can see, at a glance, the changes they made before producing the final version. You might also want to add these criteria to your writing rubric: "Shows evidence of revision of punctuation to get at meaning" and "Shows evidence of proofreading punctuation to correct possible errors."

Tell students that most writers go back and not only revise their writing for meaning, but also proofread for punctuation mistakes. Yes, mistakes—places, for example, where writers thought they had put in a comma, but somehow left it out. Places where they meant to put a period, but it's not there. Mistakes. Just check for them. No value judgments needed. We all make mistakes. It's human.

ASK CHILDREN TO WRITE BRIEF SELF-EVALUATIONS OF PUNCTUATION USE

When we ask writers to turn their attention to themselves and evaluate their work, we give them a new way to participate in their own learning. It is more telling for a child to admit ignoring periods than for us to point it out, because it shows he or she is on the way to becoming an independent writer. Since no teacher can hold students' hands through their lives and be there to point out mistakes, students need to be able to step back, look at their writing objectively, and think about how to make it better.

What about the child who just does not see anything wrong with his writing? While I have some misgivings about the value of peer conferring, I think this is a situation where a partner can help. A punctuation partner who is more skilled may open the student's eyes to the work still to be done.

ASK STUDENTS TO WRITE PLANS FOR IMPROVING THEIR PUNCTUATION

While this is related to the last point, it transcends having students note how far they have come by having them make plans for getting better. Students think of concrete things they will do to improve. For example, a child might write, "Sometimes I forget what I wanted to say. So I will reread my writing every time I write. Then I can catch mistakes right away and remember the sound I wanted my writing to have."

In general, I require students to do this evaluative work regularly. Remember, as we lead them to look at their own work, they will become better at noticing punctuation, small as it is, and in using it to serve them as writers.

Clearly, evaluating student writing involves more than just marking errors and assigning grades. As we teach children how punctuation can empower them as writers, it is important to keep them empowered by teaching them to evaluate their own writing. It is also important for us to use the information we gather from careful study of student work to plan curriculum and to plan for meeting individual needs.

Some Closing Thoughts

I n his essay, "In Praise of the Humble Comma," Pico Iyer asserts that it is often the smallest, the humblest, things that carry the greatest influence. He says, "The gods, they say, give breath and they take it away. But the same could be said—could it not?—of the humble comma. Add it to the present clause and the mind is quite literally given time to think. Take it out, if you wish, or forget it, and the mind is deprived of a resting place."

When I think of punctuation, I think of how large the little language of dots and lines looms in our attempts to understand what written language communicates by transferring spoken words to the page. When I think of the teaching of punctuation, I worry about how easy it can be for us to fall into teaching minutia, and for us to go off on punctuation tangents that rob children of some of the power we want them to have through their writing. Punctuation in and of itself has no moral or ethical good. It is not an indicator of intelligence or talent. It is merely a tool. We cannot simplify writing down to a few easily memorized and tested rules, nor equate the conventional use of punctuation with "good writing." Yes, it is true that good writers use punctuation effectively, but good writers do not only have command of written conventions. The truth is that even flawlessly punctuated writing can be downright dull, trite, obvious, or superficial. Here are some guidelines to follow as you move ahead in your punctuation work.

ALLOW TIME TO PRACTICE

Like the punch line to the old joke, "How do you get to Carnegie Hall?" apprentice writers must practice, practice, practice using punctuation. They must reread their writing every day, and use their writers' notebooks to "play around" with punctuation, the way I might play around on the violin if I were trying to learn a sonata. We allow apprentice musicians time and space to "mess around" on their instruments; apprentice cooks "mess around" in the kitchen and burn a few hamburgers before they get it right; apprentice baseball players "mess around" with their pitches or their bat swings before they even consider playing for the majors. Our apprentice writers must have that space, too.

LEARN FROM WRITERS

We also need to study punctuation ourselves, to spend some time looking at what writers actually do with it. Look at the writing of Joyce Carol Oates and Barbara Kingsolver and Toni Morrison and Rick Bass. Look under the words for how they use punctuation to get the meaning into your heart. In a way, we must apprentice ourselves to these writers. (Or for some real fun, look at some nineteenth-century writing. For example, look at the first page of *Bleak House*. One-word sentences. Sentence fragment after sentence fragment. What was Dickens thinking?) We must open our minds to more than what we were taught in school. In the "factory model" of teaching punctuation, our teachers didn't expect to produce writers; they merely wanted to make us functional writers who could write an occasional letter. There was nothing wrong with that, as far as it went. They were well meaning. They did the best with what they knew. But now we know much more, and we know that the world today is quite different from that which our teachers knew. We know we must teach to prepare our students for a world that is far beyond any we could have imagined even 15 years ago. And we also must teach them so they will experience the sheer pleasure of having a voice and having a way for that voice to be heard.

LEARN FROM EXPERTS

I recall one cold January afternoon when my friend Isoke Nia and I met in the Writing Project office to study punctuation and to think about the punctuation in our own writing. We both played with punctuation, and we both worked at it for a long time before we got the sound that we wanted. This is not because Isoke and I don't know the rules. We each have teachers from the past whispering rules in our ears. In spite of this, and in spite of our long experience as writers, we wanted to know more. So we took out Strunk and White, Fowler, and Ann Stilman—three books you must have on your shelves—and we studied what these punctuation experts said. Often it differed from what our teachers had taught us. It differed from the one-size-fits-all, no-questions-asked, no-shades-of-meaning punctuation use that we had been taught in school.

BE HONEST AND PATIENT WITH STUDENTS

Our teachers did their best, but they, for the most part, were not writers. We need to study writers, because they are the experts. We need to be honest with children, and let them uncover nuances in the use of punctuation. We must be patient with them as they try these new skills in their own nascent writing. And we must be willing to listen to them and to coach them as they learn.

Pico Iyer says, "Punctuation then is a matter of care. Care for words, yes, but also, and more important, for what the words imply. Only a lover notices the small things: the way the afternoon light catches the nape of the neck, or how a strand of hair slips out from behind an ear, or the way a finger curls around a cup. And no one scans a letter so closely as a lover, searching for its small print, straining to hear its nuances, its gasps, its sighs and hesitations, poring over the secret messages that lie in every cadence. No iron can pierce the heart with such force as a period put at just the right place, in Isaac Babel's lovely word: a comma can let us hear a voice break, or a heart. Punctuation, in fact, is a labor of love."

Teach your students to hear punctuation in their reading and writing, and you may be teaching them more about life than you imagine.

Bibliography
of Professional Books and Articles

Anderson, Carl. 2000. *How's it going? A practical guide to conferring with student writers.* Portsmouth, NH: Heinemann.

Atwell, Nancy. 1998. *In the middle: New understandings about writing, reading, and learning, second edition.* Portsmouth, NH: Heinemann.

Bomer, Randy, and Katherine Bomer. 2001. *For a better world: reading and writing for social action.* Portsmouth, NH: Heinemann.

Cambourne, Brian. 1988. *The whole story: Natural learning and the acquisition of literacy in the classroom.* New York: Scholastic.

Cambourne, Brian, and Jan Turbill. 1991. *Coping with chaos.* Portsmouth, NH: Heinemann.

Calkins, Lucy. 1994. *The art of teaching writing: new edition.* Portsmouth, NH: Heinemann.

Calkins, Lucy. 2001. *The art of teaching reading.* New York: Addison Wesley.

Calkins, Lucy. 1980. *"When children want to punctuate."* Language arts, 57, 567–573.

Calkins, Lucy, and Lydia Bellino. 1997. *Raising lifelong learners: A parent's guide.* Reading, MA: Addison Wesley.

Cordeiro, Pat. 1998. "Dora learns to write and in the process encounters punctuation." In *Lessons to share on teaching grammar in context.* Constance Weaver, ed. Portsmouth, NH: Boynton/Cook.

Fletcher, Ralph. 1993. *What a writer needs.* Portsmouth, NH: Heinemann.

Fountas, Irene C., and Gay Su Pinnell. 1996. *Guided reading: Good first teaching for all children.* Portsmouth, NH: Heinemann.

Flynn, Nick, and Shirley McPhillips. 2000. *A note slipped under the door: Teaching from the poems we love.* Portland, ME: Stenhouse.

Goodman, Kenneth. 1986. *What's whole in whole language?* Portsmouth, NH: Heinemann.

Goodman, Yetta M., Dorothy J. Watson, and Carolyn L. Burke. 1987. *Reading miscue inventory: Alternative procedures.* Katonah, NY: Richard C. Owens.

Goodman, Kenneth S., Yetta M. Goodman, and Wendy J. Hood. 1989. *The whole language evaluation book.* Portsmouth, NH: Heinemann.

Graves, Donald H. 1983. *Writing: Teachers and children at work.* Portsmouth, NH: Heinemann.

Graves, Donald H. 1994. *A fresh look at writing.* Portsmouth, NH: Heinemann.

Hall, N. 1996. "Learning about punctuation: An introduction and an overview." In N. Hall and A. Robinson, Eds. *Learning about punctuation.* Portsmouth, NH: Heinemann.

Hansen, Jane. 2001. *When writers read, second edition.* Portsmouth, NH: Heinemann.

Harwayne, Shelley. 1992. *Lasting impressions: Weaving literature into the writing workshop.* Portsmouth, NH: Heinemann.

Iyer, Pico. 1996. "In praise of the humble comma." In *In short: A collection of brief creative nonfiction*. Judith Kitchen and Mary Paumier Jones, Eds. New York: W.W. Norton.

Krashen, Stephen. 1993. *The power of reading: Insights from the research*. Englewood, CO: Libraries Unlimited, Inc.

Laminack, Lester, and Katie Wood. 1996. *Spelling in use*. Urbana, IL: NCTE.

Meek, Margaret. 1988. *How texts teach what readers learn*. Stroud, England: Thimble Press.

Murray, Donald M. 1999. *Write to learn*. Fort Worth, TX: Harcourt Brace.

Murray, Donald M. 1993. *Read to write*. Fort Worth, TX: Harcourt Brace.

Nia, Isoke Titilayo. 1999. *"Units of study in the writing workshop."* Primary voices K-6, v.8, no.1, NCTE.

Peterson, Ralph. 1992. *Life in a crowded place: Making a learning community*. Portsmouth, NH: Heinemann.

Ray, Katie Wood. 1999. *Wondrous words: Writers and writing in the elementary classroom*. Urbana, IL: NCTE.

Rosen, Lois Matz. 1998. "Developing correctness in student writing: Alternatives to the error hunt." In *Lessons to share on teaching grammar in context*. Constance Weaver, ed. Portsmouth, NH: Boynton/Cook.

Rosenblatt, Louise M. 1978. *The reader, the text, the poem: The transactional theory of the literary work*. Carbondale: Southern Illinois University Press.

Shaughnessey, Mina P. 1977. *Errors and expectations*. New York: Oxford University Press.

Short, Kathy G., Jerome C. Harste, and Carolyn Burke. 1996. *Creating classrooms for authors and inquirers, second edition*. Portsmouth, NH: Heinemann.

Smith, Frank. 1998. *The book of learning and forgetting*. New York: Teachers College Press.

Smith, Frank. 1982. *Writing and the writer*. New York: Holt, Rinehart, and Winston.

Smith, Frank. 1988. *Joining the literacy club*. Portsmouth, NH: Heinemann.

Snowball, Diane, and Faye Bolton. 1999. *Spelling K–8: Planning and teaching*. York, ME: Stenhouse.

Strong, William. 1999. "Coaching writing development: Syntax revisited, options explored." In *Evaluating writing: The role of teachers' knowledge about text, learning, and culture*. Charles R. Cooper and Lee Odell, ed. Urbana, IL: NCTE.

Weaver, Constance, ed. 1998. *Lessons to share on teaching grammar in context*. Portsmouth, NH: Boynton/Cook.

Weaver, Constance. 1996. *Teaching grammar in context*. Portsmouth, NH: Heinemann.

Weaver, Constance. 1994. *Reading process and practice: From socio-psycholinguistics to whole language*. Portsmouth, NH: Heinemann.

Wilde, Sandra. 1992. *You kan red this!* Portsmouth, NH: Heinemann.

Wilde, Sandra. 2000. *Miscue analysis made easy: Building on student strengths*. Portsmouth, NH: Heinemann.

Wilhelm, Jeffrey D. 2001. *Improving comprehension with think-aloud strategies*. New York: Scholastic.

Very Short Lists of Books With Interesting Punctuation

Most children's literature contains an interesting array of punctuation. Use whatever is in your classroom library. There are few books that have no punctuation to study. It is worthwhile not only to study how authors use punctuation in vibrant ways, but also how they balance that with a clear knowledge of conventional use. Both are important to study.

Picture Books

Title/Author/Publisher	Great for Teaching
The Goodnight Circle by Carolyn Lesser (Harcourt Brace)	dashes
Mrs. Katz and Tush by Patricia Polacco (Bantam)	ellipses, dashes
I'm in Charge of Celebrations by Byrd Baylor (Charles Scribner)	dashes, parentheses, colons
Thunder Cake by Patricia Polacco (Philomel)	ellipses, dashes
Scarecrow by Cynthia Rylant (Harcourt Brace)	apostrophes, colons, commas in lists, ellipses
Aunt Flossie's Hats (and crab cakes later) by Elizabeth Fitzgerald Howard (Clarion)	dashes, quotation marks within quotation marks
The Important Book by Margaret Wise Brown (Harper)	commas in lists
Amazing Grace by Mary Hoffman (Dial Books)	ellipses, dashes
My Mama Had a Dancing Heart by Libba Moore Gray (Orchard Books)	hyphens
Come On, Rain! by Karen Hesse (Scholastic)	ellipses, quotation marks in dialogue exchanges
Snow by Uri Shulevitz (Farrar, Straus and Giroux)	commas

Chapter Books

Title/Author/Publisher
Detective Dinosaur Lost and Found by James Skofield (HarperCollins)
Frog and Toad Together by Arnold Lobel (Harper & Row)
Henry and Mudge Under the Yellow Moon by Cynthia Rylant (Bradberry)
Amber Brown Goes Fourth by Paula Danziger (G.P. Putnam's Sons)
Fish Face by Patricia Reilly Giff (Dell)
The Beast in Ms. Rooney's Room by Patricia Reilly Giff (Dell)
Pee Wee Scouts #3, That Mushy Stuff by Judy Delton (Dell)
Autumn Street by Lois Lowry (Houghton Mifflin)
Dragonwings by Lawrence Yep (Harper & Row)
Guests by Michael Dorris (Hyperion)
The Winter Room by Gary Paulsen (Orchard Books)
Shiloh by Phyllis Reynolds Naylor (Atheneum)
The View from Saturday by E.L. Konigsburg (Atheneum)
Jacob Have I Loved by Katherine Paterson (Crowell)
Wringer by Jerry Spinelli (HarperCollins)

NAME _____ DATE _____

CLASS _____

Comment Sheet for Readers
from Other Classes

Dear Reader,

Thanks for taking the time to read my writing. It would help me become a better writer if you would answer some of the questions below. I hope you enjoyed my story!

Sincerely,

_____

Name _____ **Date** _____

Please tell me one thing you liked about this piece of writing. _____

_____

Do you think the writing is clear? If not, where is it unclear? _____

What is one thing I could do to make this story better? _____

Please tell me one way my writing made you think about your own writing. _____

Is there something you think I should write next? A sequel? A different genre? _____

_____

Do you have any other comments? _____

_____

An explanation of how to use this reproducible appears on page 29.

NAME _____ DATE _____

Reading Like Writers

Example from text	What do you notice?	Name it	Why did the author do this?	Try it! How did it go?

An explanation of how to use this reproducible appears on page 43.

NAME_____   DATE_____

Studying What
Strunk and White Say. . .
and What It Means for My Writing

	Rule #_____ Page #_____	Rule #_____ Page #_____	Rule #_____ Page #_____
What the rule says			
Examples from books I've read			
Examples from my own writing			
The rule stated in kid language			
Examples where authors break the rule and why they do it (optional)			

An explanation of how to use this reproducible appears on page 99.

NAME _____ DATE _____

Punctuation Study in Four Genres

four genres				
What I noticed about punctuation				
Example from litetature				
What this means for my writing				
Example from my writing				

An explanation of how to use this reproducible appears on page 104.

NAME _____   DATE _____

Self-Evaluation Form

Title of writing: _____

One place where I used punctuation as I wrote to help me shape meaning: _____

_____

_____

One place where I used a mentor text to help me punctuate: _____

_____

_____

The mentor text I studied and used: _____

One way I used punctuation well: _____

One way I tried to use punctuation in a new way for me: _____

_____

One aspect of punctuation that I want to work on: _____

_____

An explanation of how to use this reproducible appears on page 106.

NAME _____   DATE _____

Independent Study
Planning Sheet

Names of people in group: _____

_____

What we are studying: _____

How we plan to find out what we want to know: _____

_____

Some books we might use: _____

_____

What we are thinking and why: _____

_____

Some possible conclusions. (Fill this out as you near the end of the study.): _____

_____

718-575-2930   Dr. Charles Kleinberg
109 33 71st Rd Forest

An explanation of how to use this reproducible appears on page 119.